Communicating

A Contemporary Approach

Henry L. Roubicek

Mary Evelyn Collins

Deloris McGee Wanguri

University of Houston
Downtown Campus

Kendall/Hunt
Publishing Company

Copyright © 1986 by Kendall/Hunt Publishing Company

Library of Congress Catalog Card Number: 86-81463

ISBN 0-8403-3996-8

All rights reserved. No part of this publication may be reproduced, stored in a retrieval system, or transmitted, in any form or by any means, electronic, mechanical, photocopying, recording, or otherwise, without the prior written permission of the copyright owner.

Printed in the United States of America

B 403996 01

To Those
  Who Want
    To Get
      Better At
        Talking To
          OTHERS
           And
            Talking To
              THEMSELVES

Contents

Preface, ix

Chapter One. Communicating: The Key Ingredients, x
    Why Communicate, 1
    Communication Is Inevitable, 1
    Communication Is Difficult, 2
    Sending and Receiving, 2
        Noise, 3
        Perceptual Filters, 3
    Feedback, 5
        Feedback and Acquiring a Self Concept, 5
        Feedback and the Intrapersonal Self, 6
    Language and Meaning, 7
        Meaning, 9
        Types of Meaning, 10
    Listening, 10
        Types of Listening, 11
    Summary, 12
    Instructional Exercises, 13
    Additional Readings, 13

Chapter Two. Communicating Nonverbally, 14
    Nonverbal Communication as Coding, 16
    Movement as Language, 16
        Types of Movement, 17
    Distance as Language, 18
        Proxemic Distances, 19
    Sound as Language, 20
    Summary, 21
    Instructional Exercises, 22
    Additional Readings, 22

Chapter Three. Communicating in Relationships, 24
    Thinking about Relationships, 25
    Viewing Relationships in Economic Terms, 25
        Social Exchange, 26
        Comparison Levels, 26
    Interpersonal Needs, 27
        Viewing Relationships, 28
        Needs and Types of Relationships, 29
    On Being Assertive, 31
        Assertiveness Is Winning Communication, 31
        Results from Not Fighting for Your Fundamental Rights, 31
        What Stops Us from Being Assertive, 32
        Taking Control, 32
        Improving Skills in Assertiveness, 32
    Communication Climate, 33
    Self Disclosure, 34
        Levels of Sharing, 35
        Self Disclosure Should Be Shared and Nurtured, 36
        Keeping a Secret, 37
    Summary, 37
    Instructional Exercises, 38
    Additional Readings, 39

Chapter Four. Communicating in the Interview, 40
    Interviews Are Not Simple Events, 41
    The Interview: A Definition, 41
    Dual Roles, 42
    Types of Interviews, 43
        The Information Gathering Interview, 43
        The Employment Interview, 45
    Lawful and Unlawful Pre-Employment Inquiries, 47
    Summary, 49
    Instructional Exercises, 49
    Additional Readings, 50

Chapter Five. Communicating in the Group, 52
    What Is a Group, 53
    Types of Groups, 53
    Why Communicate in Small Groups, 54
        Functions, 54
        Advantages, 55
    The Group as a Team, 55

Decision Making, 56
    Decision-Making and Intuition, 56
    Decision-Making Is a Risk, 56
    Decisions and Outcomes, 57
    Decisions and Values, 58
Problem Solving, 58
    A Reflective Approach to Problem Solving, 59
    Monitoring Problem Solving, 59
    Brainstorming, 60
    Attitudes and the Problem Solving Group, 60
Latitude of Acceptance and Ego Involvement, 61
Leadership, 61
Roles, 62
    Role Set, 63
    Role Conflict, 63
Behavioral and Communication Concerns, 64
Summary, 65
Instructional Exercises, 66
Additional Readings, 67

Chapter Six. Communicating in the Organization, 68
    Are Organizations Important to You, 69
    Organizations: A Definition, 69
    Historical and Modern Approaches to Understanding Organizational Behavior, 71
    Organizational Socialization, 71
    Organizational Communication: A Definition, 73
    Communication Flow Within Organizations, 73
        Formal Organizational Communication, 73
        Informal Organizational Communication, 75
    Symbolic Communication Within Organizations, 76
    Barriers to Effective Organizational Communication, 77
    Techniques for Improving Organizational Communication, 78
    Summary, 79
    Instructional Exercises, 80
    Additional Readings, 81

Chapter Seven. Communicating to the Public, 82
    Audience Analysis, 84
    Physical Factors, 85
    Adjusting Topics to Purpose and Audience, 87

Data Gathering and Organization, 88
    Organization, 89
    Types of Outlines, 91
    Patterns of Organization, 92
Language and Language Use, 94
    Clarity, 95
    Conciseness, 95
    Vividness, 95
    Relevance, 96
    Language Use and Speech Purpose, 96
    Beginning the Speech, 96
    Overviews, 98
    Summaries, 98
    Ending the Speech, 98
    Special Problems with Persuasive Speeches, 99
Delivery, 99
    Building Credibility, 100
Instructional Exercises, 101
Additional Readings, 101
Index, 103

Preface

Textbooks try to do many things. The one thing this textbook does not try to do is replace the instructor. The effective instructor brings to the class much of him or herself. The effective instructor is a good communicator first. The effective instructor can communicate the knowledge gained from years of formal and private preparation. The effective instructor communicates the enthusiasm and personality developed over a lifetime of experience. And, of course, the effective instructor is a good organizer of time and materials so that the students can easily follow and relate to the content of the course.

The effective communication course, in hindsight, does something for the students. First, if the course is effective, it has approached the needs of the students currently enrolled. The effective communication course presents challenges to the students that motivates them to try out new ideas. The effective course covers the basic skills that are deemed by the Academic community as necessary for a college educated person. The effective communication course telescopes to the future so that the students learn theories, concepts, and skills that will assist them in life beyond college.

With the effective instructor and the effective course in mind, we have tried to put together an effective textbook. An effective textbook allows the instructor to create and interpret, even at times, to disagree. The effective textbook allows the instructor a data base without knowledge overkill. The effective textbook then becomes a basis for study for the student. The effective textbook does not become a substitute for the instructor. The effective textbook is not a crutch, nor is it an encyclopedia for all communication.

Communicating a contemporary approach seeks to be an effective text for the effective instructor to use in an effective course. This text relies on illustrations, examples, and anecdotes. This text seeks to promote good teaching by leaving room for lecture and personal instruction. This text does not seek to be everything to everyone. Indeed, this text may go beyond just being contemporary: this text may be considered radical.

The authors request that you instructors use the text rather than allowing the text to use you. We also request that you students rely on the instructor and the class experience itself, rather than on the text, to make the course in communication valuable for today and tomorrow.

1
Communicating: The Key Ingredients

Why Communicate?

The year is 3245 A.D. The inhabitants of the planet Earth have survived famine, pollution, wars, and a complete change in the eco-system. They have survived because of their great adaptability and intellect. Even the physical structure of the inhabitants has changed. The Earthlings have long thin bodies with large smooth heads. The head is punctuated only by two large eyes. The sense of intellect is so well developed that brain-waves, that is the way thoughts of each Earthling, are passed on to another. All they have to do is concentrate on one another. This has eliminated many problems: no more confused meanings by having to use spoken words, no more translating body language, no more confusion because groups and societies can't understand one another. There is peace because there is no longer the need for grouping, all contact is by thought.

This isn't the year 3245 A.D. We are still just plain human beings struggling to effect a peaceful, successful existence. One of the inevitable problems facing each one of us is that we need one another. We need other human beings in order to make a living, to have work that makes us feel needed and gives us a livelihood. We need others to supply us with the things that make life easier and enjoyable. We need others to keep us from the truly human emotion of loneliness. Rather than fantasize about the future, we should recognize that we must communicate with others and do it as effectively as possible. The most basic way of sending and receiving messages to one another is through our senses: seeing, hearing, touching, smelling, tasting. The best way to improve our communication skill is to start at the beginning. What is communication and why do we do it?

Communication is Inevitable

Almost every textbook in the field of speech communication discusses the fact that "one cannot not communicate." This double negative usually throws students off. One of the chief reasons that students are confused by the statement is that they confuse the notion of communication with "effective" communication. Just about everyone, at one time or another, has heard the statement, "There is a lack of communication." But the truth is: There is no such thing as a lack of communication; only a lack of effective communication. As long as messages are being sent, either to yourself, or to someone else, communication is taking place. When a teacher is lecturing, a student may not be communicating in an oral way, but that student may be communicating disinterest or boredom. Perhaps a student is daydreaming or has something else on his mind. These are communication events, even if total understanding is not shared between the key communicators (teacher and student) in the encounter.

Communication Is Difficult

Many people unfamiliar with the study of communication view communication as a mode of oral expression. Actually, oral expression, or the words used in our communication, means very little. There are over six hundred and fifty thousand words in the English language. Of these words, the average, educated adult uses only about two thousand words daily, and of those two thousand words, there are over six hundred dictionary definitions. So if we depended on words to always get our point across, we would be in trouble. What, then, are our other communicative options?

We can choose "options" to get our communication across well, but most of our communication is simply not optional. Nonverbal communication, for example, makes up most (over 75%) of our communication behavior and is typically less deceptive and more spontaneous than verbal communication. When we consider all of the nonverbal elements, and combine those with all of the verbal elements, we find ourselves experiencing one of the most difficult activities in our lives—communicating.

Sending and Receiving

Traditionally, significant emphasis has been placed on the sender of the message. This is due to the underrated importance of effectively listening (rather than hearing) to the message by the message receiver. Communication is, in fact, *reciprocal*. In any given encounter involving two or more persons, each communicator is communicating simultaneously. This is important to understand, because listening is a form of powerful talk.

For some time, people have viewed listening as a *passive-compliant* position, rather than a powerful position. After all, as an elementary school student, how many times did your teacher look at you and say, "Tommy, you look as though you are listening. I think I'll reward you with a star." Probably never. We have been told that if we want to be considered to be a successful person, open your mouth and talk, talk, talk away.

Consider the following model and its representation of communication as a reciprocal process:

Figure 1.1.
A Representation of the Communication Process

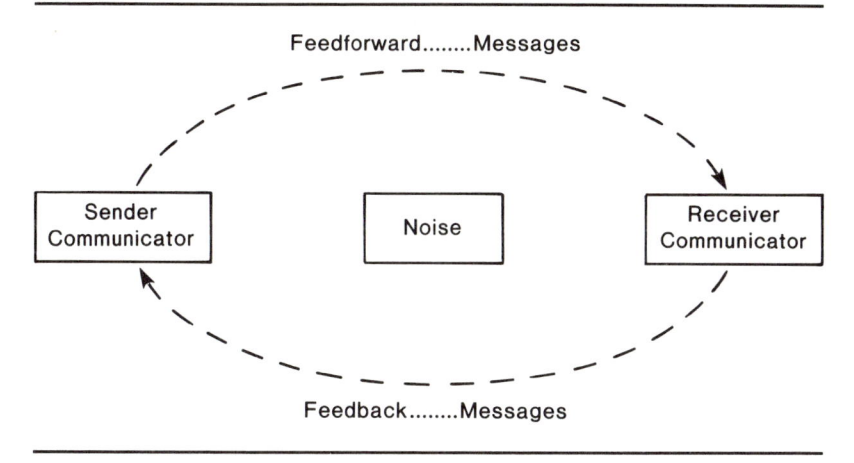

```
                    Feedforward........Messages
            ┌─────┐                    ┌─────────┐
            │Sender│        ┌─────┐    │Receiver │
            │Commu-│        │Noise│    │Commu-   │
            │nicator│       └─────┘    │nicator  │
            └─────┘                    └─────────┘
                    Feedback........Messages
```

Although a communication is initiated from a *sender,* the *receiver* of message must interpret it and send it back to the original sender, and the original sender must send it back to the receiver if the communication was not effective. The circular motion of the process identifies communication as a dynamic, on-going, never-ending process.

Noise

The key ingredient making much of our communication ineffective is *noise.* Noise, or "interference," is integral to the communication model, because noise is inevitable in the communication process. Noise can be defined as *any kind of competing stimuli which contains the smooth flow of accurate message sending and message receiving.*

Noise may take the form of listening barriers (discussed later in this chapter), daydreaming, physical and psychological distractions, environmental constraints, time of day, fatigue, frustration, stress, anxiety or language interference.

Perceptual Filters

An old philosophy professor once said to me, "What you perceive to be real, and what is real is exactly the same thing, or else you are asked to choose between two things when you only see one." At first hearing, the seemingly profound thought didn't make much sense. But later, I knew what that professor meant. He meant that people have a tendency to focus in on one thing at one time. Beyond one thing, life becomes confusing. Perception, as a possible form of noise, can help us to understand this human tendency. Perception can be defined as taking information and placing it into a coherent system of thought that makes sense to the communicator.

In fact, selectively *"screening"* information that fits in "our world" can be a significant form of noise. As communicators, we tend to focus on information that is reinforcing or rewarding to us and focus on information which can be readily retrieved from our frame-of-reference (sum total of our past experiences). There are four types of screening devices. These include: (1) *selective exposure;* (2) *selective attention;* (3) *selective interpretation;* and (4) *selective retention.* All four are based on two premises: That people tend to focus on information that is reinforcing and/or rewarding to them; and that people will draw from their frame-of-reference when engaged in informational screening.

Selective exposure is a *prediction that the message one will be focusing on will be reinforcing or rewarding.* When students begin college, they rarely know for which career they would be best suited. Nevertheless, choices are frequently made. One might desire medicine, the other law, still another might want to pursue a career in sales. These students have never been in those professions, but perhaps from having a role model, or through encouragement, or even from a "gut" feeling, these students predict the profession in which they would like to be exposed. Some of us choose our instructors through selective exposure. We talk to our friends, especially those who have taken courses with certain teachers, and ask them, "Is he easy?" "Is she fair?" Or "How many books will I need to buy for his course?" We get the necessary information and selectively expose ourselves to a course or professor.

Selective attention occurs when we are *presented by two or more pieces of information simultaneously and forced to focus on the information that is most rewarding and/or reinforcing to us.* Say, for instance, you just bought a new Ford Pinto. You open a magazine and on one side of the page you see an ad for a Ford Pinto. On the opposite side of the page you see an ad for a Chevy Chevette. Which ad will you focus on? You will probably focus on the ad for the Pinto because you just spent your hard earned money on that car. You do not want to find out that the Chevette may have been a better buy. That would not be rewarding to you, or reinforce you as a "smart" consumer.

Selective interpretation occurs *when we see things the way we want to see them.* For example, every student takes notes in class, yet notes are taken in different ways. Some students jot down definitions, others focus on examples and illustrations, and others may take no notes at all. This selection process can cause problems when studying for an exam. Have you ever been tempted to walk up to your professor and say, "This exam question is unfair because it wasn't in my notes." Perhaps your professor was at fault. But it is most likely a problem in interpreting classroom information the way you would like to interpret it, rather than the way the information needed to be interpreted.

Selective retention is based on the principle *that we remember things the way we want to remember them.* This screening process occurs in every kind of communication context. It is especially common in interpersonal encounters. Consider this: You want to break off your relationship with your girl/boy friend. You are walking with him or her on the beach, carefully discussing the need to end the relationship, and your "friend" turns to you and says, "What do you mean you want to break up. Don't you remember when we walked the same beach five years ago, and you told me how much you loved me?" This person is selectively remembering an incident that will hopefully help you change your mind. After all, breaking up the relationship may be rewarding to you, but it would be unrewarding to your friend.

Sometimes, all four screening devices take place in a communication event. An assessment of how the devices affected the event can help determine the effectiveness of the event. Consider a course taken in college. A student chooses to expose himself or herself to a course, or by enforcing a requirement, a college may expose a student to a course (selective exposure). The same student attends to multiple stimuli (selective attention) and interprets the information (selective interpretation). If a student remembers significant course information well after the course has been completed (selective retention), then perhaps the course could be viewed as a good investment of time and energy.

Feedback

Feedback is a vital ingredient in the communication process. It means, simply, the messages one receives from another. Although this definition sounds easy enough to understand, it means a great deal more. There is a difference between feedback and constructive feedback. Feedback is common, but so is bad communication. Constructive feedback is the kind of feedback that helps one to modify his or her behavior. Constructive feedback is an important step toward promoting effective communication.

Feedback and Acquiring a Self Concept

There are three forms of feedback that we receive from others: (1) *confirmation;* (2) *rejection;* and (3) *disconfirmation.* These forms of feedback help shape our self-concepts. Confirmation occurs *when an individual, especially a "significant" individual, accepts the definition that one has given to himself.* If you perceive yourself as being an "A" student, and you receive an "A" on an exam, then the teacher has accepted the definition that you gave to yourself. This form of feedback is quite constructive. It makes a person feel good, confident and worthwhile.

Interestingly enough, rejection can also be constructive feedback. If you perceive yourself to be an "A" student and receive a "C" on an exam, the instructor *may not have accepted the definition that you have given yourself,* but may be providing you with vital information that will enable you to improve or "modify" your behavior. You may perceive the incident as rejection, but it may be constructive feedback.

For the most part, however, rejection is destructive. It is a kind of feedback which can make a person feel worthless, alienated and lonely. When we ask someone out on a date, we run the risk of being rejected. Most of the time we overcome that sort of rejection. But a malicious attempt to reject someone can be quite destructive. Telling a person that he or she is an idiot, worthless, ugly, incompetent, stupid or the like, is almost always unwarranted, and can result in tragic consequences. Remember, people help people to shape their self-concepts. We need to do whatever is necessary to help persons maintain healthy self-concepts.

Although rejection is usually destructive, disconfirmation is the worst possible kind of message. If you perceive yourself to be an "A" student, and you don't receive any exam back, you have no idea what definition your instructor is giving you. You feel ignored. Feeling ignored can have disastrous effects on people. Psychotherapeutic literature suggests that people who are constantly disconfirmed by others may, after a period of time, question their own identity. Cases of verbal child abuse make the point well: Consider the story of the little girl sitting up on her bed in the middle of the night screaming, "Mommy, mommy, I'm thirsty." The mother, angered by the interruption responds with, "No you are not. Shut-up and go back to sleep." Mommy is telling her little girl that she is not experiencing what she thinks she's experiencing.

Disconfirming is a form of feedback *that causes people to value themselves less.* A person who is disconfirming someone is rejecting both the communicator and what he or she has to say. Disconfirmation is a type of feedback that is never constructive.

Feedback and the Intrapersonal Self

Talking to yourself is really a healthy thing. When you talk to yourself, or argue with yourself, you can never lose. *Intrapersonal communication,* or communicating with yourself, is commonly viewed as the first form of communication ever experienced. This is not the case. The first mode of communication experienced in life is interpersonal communication, or communication between two people.

Even before we are born, we communicate with our mothers through *tactile* (touching) communication. From that point on, our interactions with others either directly or indirectly shape our frame-of-reference, and as a result, we acquire an intrapersonal self. Even when we dream (intrapersonal event), we dream about things that were stimulated and created in our thoughts by others. We dream about bills that haven't been paid, problems with our parents, an illness in our family, sexual problems with our mate and other thoughts promoted by significant others around us.

Significant others can also help us to identify our "real" and "ideal" selves. Our real self *consists of concrete information about us which helps us to answer questions such as Who we are? What are our strengths and limitations? Where are we vulnerable?* Our ideal self *consists of more nebulous information compelling us to ask such questions as "What kind of person will I marry?" "Will I be able to get a better job?" "How might I get into a position of power?"*

Sometimes, a person might possess too much ideal self and not enough real self. This dilemma of self can be illustrated by the student who confidently strolls by his adviser's office, sticks his head in and says, "I'll stop by next week to work on my fall schedule. I don't want to take any biology, chemistry or math, because I'm miserable in those subjects. I don't like being around people much, so be ready to suggest some classes for me with small enrollments. I need to do well this semester because I plan on becoming a cardiovascular surgeon." This student's adviser is going to need to have a "reality of self" discussion with his advisee. Clearly, this student is more concerned with the prestige of becoming a doctor than with dealing with his "real" limitations in becoming one.

Conversely, a person with too much real self and very little ideal self may lack the ability to dream, fantasize and hope for the future. This person will probably not want to take many risks. He may think that if he takes risks, failure will inevitably follow. This person will probably end up swimming in a pool of mediocrity, instead of trying to "follow his dreams."

As one might imagine, a balance of real and ideal self is worth struggling for. Through effective communication with others, we learn to be more self-aware and self-accepting. We learn to appreciate the support and understanding that we receive from the significant others around us. We also learn to accept criticism from those who can help us to improve. It is important to remember: Our intrapersonal self is made up of communication events encountered with others. The healthier our communication is with others, the healthier the communication is within ourselves.

Language and Meaning

Since human beings must communicate, humankind has found the use of oral and written language a means to more easily communicate one to another. We usually take language for granted, giving little thought to what language is and how we acquired it. We may run into confusion because of mixed up meanings, but we rarely stop to figure out why we have a problem with meaning.

Early in the history of language, communicators used a type of sign language along with early sounds to "talk" with one another. If the communicator, or sender of the message, wanted a more permanent message, pictures were drawn to convey the message. These small pictures represented the persons, places, and things in the message. Although this seems primitive to us now, we would revert to the same methods if we found ourselves face to face with another person who spoke no English and we did not speak her language. We would probably use all types of gestures, or primitive sign language, or even draw pictures to get our message across. Even though we are in control of a very complex language, if we do not share the same *system* of *symbols* we are lost.

You have probably heard the old saying "a rose by any other name is still a rose." What this means is that the actual flower with soft petals and a thorny stem remains the same, no matter what we call it. In this respect, language is arbitrary; that is, the *symbol for the thing being talked about is a label which does not possess any of the characteristics of the thing itself.* Names are arbitrary. "Oh, you don't look like a Kim," means to the person, Kim, that the speaker has another image of what a "Kim" looks like. What does a Kim look like? Is there a standard description? Are children assigned names based on certain characteristics they possess? Typically we are named whatever our parents want to name us . . . that is *arbitrariness.*

Not all words are symbols for things. Human language has the capacity to code abstractions. We can talk about emotions, feelings, pain, the past, the present, and the future. *The ability to talk about things in the past or future, or things removed from us by distance is called displacement.* We can talk about things far away from our locale. We can make descriptions of things we have not seen because of the qualities of abstraction and displacement.

Our language also links us with others who share our symbol system. I was standing in a check-out line in a grocery on Avenue A on the Lower East Side in Manhattan. As I was standing I politely smiled at the older lady behind me in the line. She immediately began to speak in a language that could have been jibberish, for all I knew. I politely said, "Pardon, me," smiling again. Immediately, the lady said in English, "Oh, I am so sorry. I thought you were Polish." I don't know what she said, but it sounded friendly. We learn the language of our first family unit. Along with the language comes the cultural content necessary to relate to those in that culture. Had I been brought up in a Polish home, I would have learned Polish. Obviously I look enough like a Pole that I would have had no problem fitting in. No matter the national or cultural origin of a child, it learns its language from those who nurture it as it grows.

Spoken language has some unique characteristics. The spoken word is almost *spontaneous.* We often speak without much time lapse between the stimulus and our response. This gives spoken language the aura of *creativity* and *productivity,* other than the habitual utterances, such as "Hi! How are you?" "OK. How are you?" We utter language as we are thinking. We have not been programmed ahead to say things on cue. This also means that this creativity affects our ability to come up with new symbols. As symbol users, we can create new symbols to suit our needs as communicators.

Within the shared system of symbols there are sub-systems of symbols that are used by sub-group who use the large system and the sub-system as well. Not every system user can, or would want to use all the sub-systems. Here are some of the types of sub-systems.

1. *Jargon is the label used to designate the sub-system used by members of a professional group.* The language in jargon describes a concept or thing that is recognized by others in that field. Jargon only confuses those who are not a part of the subgroup using the particular subsystem. However, jargon can become a part of the larger system, if the number of people using the jargon increase to a wide number of the population. An

example of this would be the generalized use of computer-language by the main population.
2. *Slang is the label used to designate the subsystem used in very casual or street conversation.* The origins of slang words are diverse. With the advent of mass media, especially the broadcast media, slang symbols have at times entered the larger symbol system.
3. *Argot is the label used to designate the subsystem used by nonprofessionals.* This is not the same as jargon, since the subgroup may not represent a particular set of professionals. A good example of argot is the language used by CB radio operators. Symbols in cant sometimes become slang.
4. *Cant is the label used to designate the subsystem used by the criminal or underworld subculture, such as thieves, drug dealers, prostitutes, and street gangs.* Outsiders are usually unable to understand the language, because it deliberately seeks to cloak, or hide, the meanings.

Meaning

Each symbol has a meaning. In fact, the symbol may have more than one meaning. How does a symbol get a meaning? The symbol itself does not generate a meaning, because the symbol was arbitrarily assigned. The meaning of the symbol is made in the mind of the symbol user.

C. K. Ogden and I. A. Richards in 1923 developed a theory of meaning. They suggested that there were three main areas to observe in the development of meaning. First, there is the object itself, called the *Referent.* Then there is the *Symbol,* or the label for the Referent. Then there is the *Reference,* or the thought of the symbol user. Ogden and Richards diagrammed the relationship of these three areas of meaning as follows:

Figure 1.2.
Relationships of Meaning

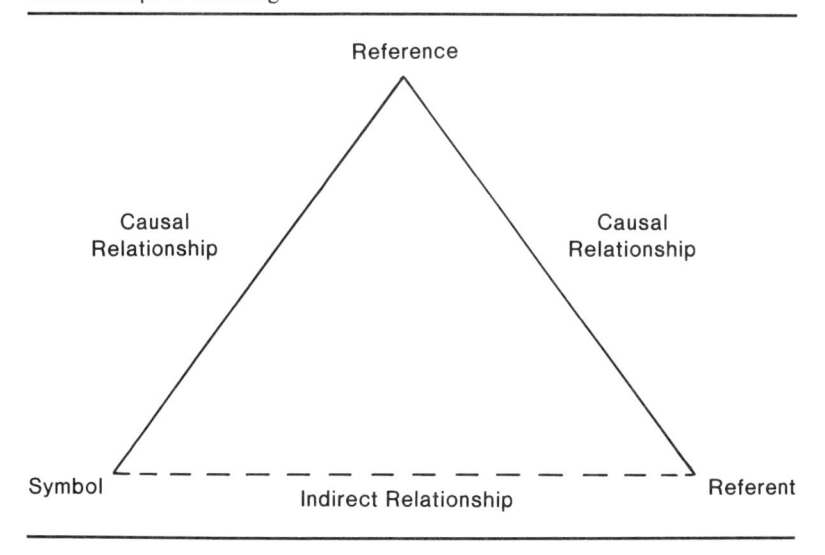

The relationship between the thought of the symbol-user and the symbol and the symbol-user and the object is a causal, or direct, relationship. However, the symbol and the object have an indirect and arbitrary relationship. That is, something has caused the symbol user to place certain meaning in the symbol when stimulated by the object.

Types of Meaning

There are two broad categories for the kinds of meanings of symbols that we use: *denotative* and *connotative* meanings.

First, *denotative meanings are those meanings which we can agree on, are widely accepted, and end up in dictionaries.* Denotative meanings are specific. A denotative meaning is not an emotional meaning. For example, the word marriage in the denotative sense means the ceremony and process of two people living as husband and wife. The word itself might bring to mind many emotional visions, but these are not within the denotative meaning.

The emotional and personal meanings people give to symbols are their connotative meanings. Certain symbols can have shared emotional meanings within subgroups. An example would be the symbol "war" with a group of veterans. Someone who had not experienced the same type of war or any war at all could not feel the same as those who have had a common experience.

Listening

Much of our communication time is spent, not in the sending of messages, but in the receiving of them. When we are in the oral/aural channel of communication, that is, the mouth to ear channel, we rely heavily on our ability to listen to be an effective part of the communication process. The ability to hear and to understand are important to us.

First, we must understand that it is not enough just to hear. *Hearing is the physiological function of receiving sound waves.* If we hear, we have received the sound from the source, but hearing does not denote an ability to even marginally understand what we have heard. Listening, on the other hand, denotes some sort of understanding process is taking place. Andrew D. Wolvin and Carolyn Gwynn Coakley in their book, *Listening,* identified sixteen different proposed definitions for listening covering scholarship from 1925 to 1979. Just the fact that it is difficult to point out one definition for listening indicates that the process is a complex one.

Almost all proposed definitions for the term *listening* has at its core the intake of sound (hearing) and the mental processing of those sounds into meaningful mental images. Some definitions suggest that listening requires some memory of what is heard. This could be long or short-term memory. It is safe to use the following definition: *listening is the taking in of sound, which can be a structured message from a sender, and processing that sound mentally into meaningful thought, which will be retained in long or short-term memory.*

Types of Listening

Florence Wolff, Nadine Marsnik, William Tacey, and Ralph Nichols, in *Perceptive Listening,* list four basic types of listening:

1. discriminative listening
2. evaluative listening
3. appreciative listening
4. empathic listening.

These four basic types have their origin in the reasons why we listen. The listener plays a different role in each type of listening.

Discriminative listening is the type of listening we do when we have a specific need to know the information being given to us. When we go to class to learn about a subject from the professor, we are listening discriminatively. When the telephone representative explains all the different ways we can have long distance service, we are listening discriminatively. There is a certain amount of concentration, especially on the outline of thought used by the speaker. An effective listener in this situation would also try to think of questions to ask the speaker in order to better understand what has been said.

Evaluative listening is the type of listening we do when we are given persuasive messages. The speaker is trying to get us to change our thinking, our action, our daily behavior, our attitudes, even the way we spend our money. The process of persuasion is very complex; therefore we must be aware that we are receiving the efforts of a persuader. A persuader must get our attention first, then present us with a believable description of his direction, then present valued evidence. The effective listener will quickly assess the speaker's reasoning pattern and the quality of the evidence being presented. The listener should be able to recognize weaknesses in the reasoning process and question those areas that are not understandable. The effective listener should be able to determine whether or not the speaker has succeeded in the persuasion process: were you persuaded?

Appreciative listening is the listening we do when we are seeking enjoyment, pleasure, or cultural enlightenment. Appreciative listening brings about an enriched quality in our lives. The best way to improve your appreciative listening skills is to set aside time to do it. Give yourself time to take in the sounds that give you pleasure and enhance your life. As you become more experienced as an appreciative listener, you will be able to more quickly identify the listening we like most. An effective listener does not rule out sources of appreciative listening, therefore taking on new listening challenges and increasing the ability to process new sounds, words, ideas, and thoughts.

Empathic listening is the type of listening we do when others need to talk to someone who will listen. Rather than gaining from empathic listening, we are actually giving understanding to the speaker. "Empathic" comes from the word "empathy" which denotes a sense of feeling "with" a person, rather than feeling "toward" them. This implies that there is a shared experience involved in the feeling of empathy. When we give our attention to the speaker we begin to focus on her words and feelings. If we give the speaker time we will begin to realize that we can empathize with her. The key is to give time with an open mind. A judgmental clock watcher is not an effective empathic listener.

Summary

As we have seen, communication is inevitable. The human organism must communicate with others. We use both verbal and nonverbal "options" to get our message to receivers.

During the process of receiving messages we use four screen devices: selective exposure; selective attention; selective interpretation; and selective retention. These screening devices can become significant forms of noise, that is, barriers to communication.

Feedback is the messages that one receives from another. We receive three forms of feedback from others: confirmation, rejection, and disconfirmation. Each type of feedback informs us about ourselves and gives us a certain amount of personal image. Confirmation makes us feel worthwhile, confident, and good. Rejection can be very destructive, making a person feel worthless, alienated, and lonely.

Intrapersonal communication is communication with self. This is a very healthy thing to do. Significant others help us to mold how we feel about ourselves. We begin to learn the differences between the "ideal" and the "real" self. The "real" self is the concrete part of the person that understands the limitations of the self and the strengths of the self. The "ideal" self helps the person to identify the hopes, dreams and aspirations of the self.

Language is acquired from those who nurture us. We begin to be able to function in the shared symbol system in our culture very early. As symbol users we are able to create new symbols, create new language, and become a part of sub-systems of the larger language. There are four basic types of sub-systems: jargon, slang, argot, and cant.

Meaning in language comes from the use of language. People give symbols their meaning. There are two basic types of meaning, denotative and connotative. Denotative is the specific and generally agreed upon meaning that appears in the dictionary. The connotative meaning is the emotional or personal meaning we give a symbol, or word, that comes from our experience.

Much of our communication time is spent listening. A good definition of listening is the taking in of sound, which can be a structured message from a sender, and processing that sound mentally into meaningful thought, which will be retained in long or short-term memory.

Wolf, Marsnik, Tacey, and Nichols identified four basic types of listening: discriminative listening, evaluative listening, appreciative listening, and empathic listening. We do discriminative listening when we have a need to know information. We do evaluative listening when someone is trying to persuade us. We do appreciative listening when we wish to relax and listen for enjoyment of cultural understanding. We do empathic listening whe[n] to give the speaker the opportunity to be heard because we sense that [need] to be listened to.

Instructional Exercises

1. Form a group of 6 to 10 persons. Have one person stand away from the group. The group should sit in a circle with eyes closed. The member standing away from the group should make various sounds at various distances: dropping a coin, sighing, walking, humming. As each person can hear, hold up a hand.
2. Have a member of the class read a news story for about five minutes. Take a short "test" to see how much you remember.
3. Have members in the class introduce themselves and then ask someone to name members.
4. Play "gossip." Start by whispering a sentence with one member of the class and go around. What is the result? Who had the most difficulty?

Additional Readings

Barker, Larry L. *Listening Behavior.* Englewood Cliffs, N.J.: Prentice-Hall, 1971.

Berlo, David K. *The Process of Communication.* New York: Holt, Rinehart and Winston, 1960.

Goffman, Erving. *The Presentation of Self in Everyday Life.* Garden City, N.Y.: Doubleday (Anchor Books), 1959.

Keetner, John W. *Interpersonal Speech Communication: Elements and Structures.* Belmont, Cal.: Wadsworthy, 1970.

Nichols, Ralph G., and Stevens, Leonard. *Are You Listening?* New York: McGraw-Hill, 1957.

[handwritten note: For clients — What is the purpose of your communication need? — In other words what & why do you need to communicate?]

2
Communicating Nonverbally

The rain is coming down. Your bus is late, but you continue to stand on the corner. Finally you see the bus coming. The closer it gets, the faster it seems to go. Then you realize that the driver feels the bus is too full to stop for you. As you watch it go by, with umbrella in one hand and a briefcase in the other, you pucker your face and stamp your foot. The next day the bus driver tells you how sorry he was to leave there, since you are a regular rider. He adds, "I could tell you were really upset about having to wait for the next bus."

The driver only saw you as he whizzed by; how did he know you were upset?

You go to church one Sunday morning with your mother. At the end of the service your mother insists on going out the front to shake hands with the minister. Since your mother knows lots of people and loves to take her time getting out of the church, stopping to speak to many friends, the two of you are among the last to leave the church. The minister, a very friendly and outgoing person that you really like, is still shaking hands and smiling and speaking to each person. As you shake hands with him you come away feeling that maybe he should go home and rest during the afternoon.

How did you get the feel that the minister was tired?

Your roommate comes in from a date with her longstanding boyfriend and says matter of fact that they are to be married next summer. You are not sure what to say. Inside you feel that your roommate is not excited at all and may just be getting engaged to "be engaged."

Why do you feel this, since she said so little?

As we noted in Chapter One, about 75 percent of our time is spent in *nonverbal communication*. Many students think of nonverbal communication as merely "body language." Nonverbal communication includes all those channels of communication that do not select word symbols. Let's look at the examples above. Obviously, your bus driver read your stamping foot and puckered face to mean that you did not appreciate being left in the rain. He saw your message and knew how you felt without exchanging words. You sensed how exhausted your minister was even though his voice did not give him away. His handshake was hot, sweaty, and a little limp. You could tell how he felt by the touch of his hand. Your roommate told you the right words concerning her engagement, but it was the lack of enthusiasm that made you get the impression that her heart wasn't in the engagement. It wasn't the words she said, but the way she said them that cued your response. These are all examples of communicating nonverbally.

Nonverbal Communication as Coding

Nonverbal communication is just one more way to get a message to a receiver. Just as words are symbols for objects, emotions, or ideas, *nonverbal communication coding is an encoding process.* We develop abilities to encode nonverbally from the time we developed fetuses in our mother's womb. Remember in Chapter One we discussed the tactile communication an unborn child has with its mother. New born babies begin letting their parents know very quickly when they are tired, hungry, hot, cold, wet, or ill. All of these messages are given without the benefit of spoken words. Nonverbal communication is so basic that we see strong nonverbal implications in the area of interpersonal communication, organizational communication, and small group communication.

Movement As Language

Ray Birdwhistell, an anthropologist interested in linguistics, pioneered the area of nonverbal communication when he began to study *kinesics,* or body movement. Birdwhistell felt that communication makes use of all channels of our senses. His theories place emphasis on all channels rather than studying just one channel at a time. There are seven basic assumptions that Birdwhistell lists as the bases of his theory:

1. Like other events in nature, no body movement or expression is without meaning in the context in which it appears.
2. Like other aspects of human behavior, body posture, movement, and facial expression are patterned and, thus, subject to systematic analysis.
3. While the possible limitation imposed by particular biological substrata are recognized, until otherwise demonstrated, the systematic body motion of the members of a community is considered a function of the social system to which the group belongs.
4. Visible body activity, like audible acoustic activity, systematically influences the behavior of other members of any particular group.
5. Until otherwise demonstrated such behavior will be considered to have an investigable communicational function.
6. The meanings derived therefrom are functions both of the behavior and the operations by which it is investigated.
7. The particular biological system and the special life experience of any individual will contribute idiosyncratic elements to his kinesic system, but the individual or symptomatic quality of these elements can only be assessed following the analysis of the larger system of which he is a part. (from Birdwhistell, Ray. *Kinesics and Context.* Philadelphia: University of Pennsylvania Press, 1970, pp. 183–84.)

What these seven assumptions do is to help those studying body movement as language to look at the body movement as a part of a system of symbols that have meaning. *Assumption one* states that body movements and expressions always have a meaning, when you look at them in context. That is, they don't stand alone, but are a part of a communication situation. The *second assumption* merely states that we move in patterns, or we have habituated our movements and gestures to suit our system of communication. The *third assumption* states that even with some limitations, the systematic body movement of members of a community group is a part of the socialization process of that group. That is to say, that the gestures we use, the body motions that we have are directly influenced by the socialization of the group. *Assumption four* is very closely related to the third, because the body movements of a member of a group can influence the behavior of other members of the group. *Assumption five* states that since the body movement behavior of a group is systematic and functional, then the body movement should be studied. The *sixth assumption* states that by studying the movement of the body, meaning can be derived from the functional use of the movements, and the procedures used to study the movement also influence how we view the meanings. The *seventh assumption* merely states that no matter how individualized the body movement characteristics of a person, those characteristics still fit into the larger communication system in which he participates.

Types of Movement

Through the study of kinesics there have been found a number of types of movement that can be categorized from observing movement and general behavior of communicators. Paul Edman and Wallace Friesen suggested five basic types of movement:

1. adaptors
2. emblems
3. illustrators
4. affect displays
5. regulators.

Adaptors are nonverbal behaviors that *we* perform in private. These behaviors are sometimes seen in public when the *person* is either oblivious to being in public, or is not indoctrinated in public behavior. An example would be scratching or rubbing the body. We usually wait to perform these behaviors until we are in private, but we often try to covertly scratch if we just can't wait.

Object adaptors are nonverbal behaviors that use an object or prop to do the behavior. An example of this is the man who lights a cigarette and rather than smoking it seems to use it as a part of his hand to gesture. Another example is using a pen to tap on the table rather than just writing with it.

Emblems are movements, gestures, and behaviors that are actually translatable into words. For example, when someone goes out to the interstate highway, bag in hand, and sticks up his thumb, what he or she is saying to those passing by is "Please give me a ride." When Winston Churchill held up two fingers in a "V" he was saying "Victory."

Illustrators are the movements and behaviors that go along with a verbal message. These movements actually "illustrate" what is being said, sort of like a picture to go along with the text of the message. When your date is tired and wants to leave the party, he will often say aloud, "Come on. It's time to go." Just as he is saying "Come on," he waves his hand toward the door. The waving of the hand is illustrating what he wants to do, leave.

Affect displays are facial expressions that actually show emotion. Grimacing, lifting eyebrows, puckering the face or lips, and other movements are all a part of affect display. When you have arrived home at three in the early morning and present yourself at breakfast at four or five hours later, you immediately know what your mother thinks of your late arrival by looking at her face. Her affect display tells you her feelings and you will react to her accordingly.

Distance as Language

Proxemics is the study of distance and space. We learn how to use space and distance automatically by observing and participating in the culture around us. The use of space is cultural; that is, depending upon the location of our upbringing we will use space and distance in certain ways. Edward T. Hall has been influential in the study of proxemics. From his study he suggests eight categories of proxemic behaviors:

1. postural-sex identifiers
2. sociofugal-sociopetal orientation
3. kinesthetic factors
4. touch
5. vision
6. thermal factors
7. loudness
8. smell.

Postural-sex identifiers refer to the posture and the sex of the sender and the receiver of the message. The sub-categories of the postural-sex identifiers refer to the position and posture of the communicators: man prone, woman prone, man sitting or squatting, woman sitting or squatting, man standing, and woman standing.

Sociofugal-sociopetal orientation category includes the specification of the relationship of one person's shoulders to the other person's shoulders. There are nine positions of the shoulder's classified by Hall: face to face, 45 degree angle, 90 degree angle, 135 degree angle, 180 degree angle, 225 degree angle, 270 degree angle, 315 degree angle, and back-to-back. The face-to-face and back-to-back positions indicate that the shoulders are in a parallel position to one another.

Kinesthetic factors are those factors that signify the closeness of two communicators that would engender holding, grasping, or touching one another. Hall subdivided kinesthetic factors into the range of closeness: within body-contact distance, within touching distance with the forearm extended, within touching distance with the arm extended, and within touching distance by reaching.

Touch refers to the amount of actual body contact between two persons. Hall uses a seven point scale to evaluate the amount of touching that occurs between the two: caressing and holding, caressing and feeling, extending holding, holding, spot touching, brushing or accidental touching, and no contact. Clearly, these points on the scale show amount or quantity.

Vision refers to the amount of visual contact between two persons. Hall divides vision into four categories: sharp, focused looking at the other person's eyes; clear, focused looking at the other's face or head; peripheral, looking at the other person in general but not focused on the head; and no visual contact.

Thermal factors give recognition to the fact that body heat is perceived by others. Hall uses four categories to describe the perception of body heat in another person: detection of conducted heat, detection of radiant heat, probable detection of kind of heat from other person, and no detection of heat.

Loudness refers to the loudness of the person's voice. This is usually called vocal volume. Again Hall has a seven point scale for rating the loudness of a voice: silent, very soft, soft, normal, somewhat above normal, and very loud.

Smell refers to the olafactory sensations that are perceived by one person of another person. Others perceive odors about our bodies, even when we are clean and unperfumed. Hall classed the perception of odor into five types: detection of differentiated body odor, detection of undifferentiated odor, detection of breath odor, probable detection of some odor, and no detection.

Hall's categories seem very common sensical when we realize that each area is part of the problem of interrelating with others. The purpose of the categories is to assist in the study of the type and amount of nonverbal communication that occurs in any interaction.

Proxemic Distances

Hall also suggests four basic types of distance in which we operate. When we realize that there are conventions that we follow when we speak or interact with others, we see that one of the most ingrained conventions we have is the convention of space. We don't walk up to just anyone, any time, and stand within twelve inches of him. When we have to crowd on to an elevator and have to stand close to others, we tend to objectify the experience. That is, we don't look directly at the persons crowded on each side of us. Usually, we stare at the floor, or the lights over the elevator door. We know that we are in someone's "face" without permission.

Hall has four categories of space:

1. intimate
2. personal
3. social
4. public.

Intimate space is that area that we feel belongs to us. It is from six to eighteen inches from our bodies. Inside this space we take in others to caress, make love, comfort, show affection, and share secrets. We like to choose those who enter this space. Sometimes we agree to get into each other's space, such as, in contact sports or in sharing a crowded elevator or a crowded subway. We are often very cautious sharing intimate space in public.

Personal space extends beyond intimate space, extending from eighteen inches to 2.5 feet, in the close phase of personal space, to 4 feet, in the far phase. In the close phase we can extend our arms and take people into our personal space. One person can touch the other by reaching out the arm. At this distance we can see the person in detail: we can touch, perceive odor, and feel body heat. Even at four feet we have very clear perception of the other person. At the far side of personal space each person has to extend arms in order to touch.

Social distance is from 4 to 12 feet. At these distances we lose some of the detail of the other person. From 4 to 7 feet we carry on informal transactions, such as purchasing items, talking at a social gathering, sitting across the coffee table talking. In the farther range of this space, we have formal transaction. We keep our distance, so to speak, because we feel that it is expected, such as watching a famous or important person walk by. In this situation, we tend to give space.

Public distance is from 12 to 25 feet away. This is the distance we put between us and others in a very public situation. An example of this would be when we put distance between us and a crying baby on the bus. We do not want to be close, and only extenuating factors will get us closer. If we notice people filling an empty auditorium, usually they will begin by sitting way apart from one another. The first ones in the auditorium, unless they know one another, will pick out a seat well away from anyone else. Others entering the hall will have to fill in the space, but will also choose the most distant positions first.

Sound as Language

Remember the roommate who doubted her friend's engagement because of the "way" she said she was getting married? That roommate was evaluating the *paralinguistics* of her friend, that is the sound given to the words.

Each voice is different, so different in fact that voice patterns can now be used as evidence in court. Your voice has a unique quality. With that voice you can make a wide variety of sounds. If you sing you already know the range of pitches you can produce. If you have ever cheered at a football game you know how loud your voice can get. All these qualities and others make up the paralinguistic qualities of your voice.

The term *paralinguistics* comes from the fact that linguistics is the study of words, symbols. The prefix "para" signifies that there is something additional, or even assisting the main stem. Paralinguistics is the study of the sounds that are made by the voice to assist in the making of meaning for the spoken symbol.

We have many possibilities for paralinguistic study. The *rate,* for example, *is the speed at which you utter the words.* The *tempo is the rhythm at which you speak.* The *pitch is the highness or lowness perceived in your voice. Articulation is your ability to make the sounds that are* put together to make the syllable and then the word. Each one of these qualities you can observe by tape recording yourself. Each one can be adjusted and used to change intended meaning.

Other qualities of paralinguistic production include *volume, resonance,* and *phonation. Volume is the loudness of the voice. Resonance is the quality of fullness that the voice has because the vibrations have been amplified inside the body. Phonation is the ability to produce sound, that is, actually use the lungs, throat, larynx, pharynx, sinus cavity, mouth cavity, and lips to form raw sound.*

Besides these qualities, we have the addition of extra sounds, sometimes called *vocal segregates* that come into our speech. We sometimes think of these as useless sounds, such as "uh," "huh," and pauses with no sound. Actually using pauses can be very communicative. Just think of the time a boyfriend or girlfriend said, "I have something important to tell you," and then paused. That pause began to mean numerous things as it grew longer.

Other non-words enter our speech, such as laughing, crying, sighing, moaning, whining, yawning, or even belching. Adding a chuckle to a sentence can alter the meaning of the words of the sentence for those listening.

Actors give much time to the study of how to say words. Effective speakers also practice the skill of knowing how to put emphasis using volume or whisper to stress a point. Most of us do not wish to sound like a pompous actor when we speak, but we also do not wish to sound like a programmed computer voice either. Effective paralinguistics comes from practice.

Summary

Nonverbal communication is a type of coding, using channels other than spoken or written words. The movements and distance we use add or detract from the message we wish to send. Even factors such as body heat, body odor, and touch can be used to enhance messages. We can also observe nonverbal behaviors in others in order to better understand the messages sent to us.

In order to understand that the word is not just the WORD, we have to understand that, in spoken language, the characteristics of voice that are used to speak the words also give meaning to the actual symbol.

Instructional Exercises

1. Keep a diary of the nonverbal movements that you observe in others. Make sure that each entry is labelled with the context of the communication and a description of the movement. Keep the diary for a week; then present it to your instructor.
2. Using Hall's types of movements, try to keep a checklist of all the different "moves" you make during a single day. Select a partner and do the same for that person, letting the other keep track of your moves.
3. Make a list of every pleasant voice you hear in one day. Write down the time you heard the voice, give a description of it. Try to answer the question "Why do I like this voice?"
4. Sing "Old McDonald Had a Farm" with a group from your communication class. Sing it several times trying to change the mood each time you sing it: gloomy, joyous, romantic, patriotic.
5. Get a tape recorder and a newspaper. Try to read a selected article with as much meaning as possible. Play the tape back. Listen for the types of paralinguistic qualities that add to the meaning of the reading.

Additional Readings

Birdwhistell, Ray. *Introduction to Kinesics.* Louisville: University of Louisville Press, 1952.

———. *Kinesics and Context.* Philadelphia: University of Pennsylvania Press, 1970.

Burgoon, Judee K. "Nonverbal Communication Research in the 1970's: An Overview." In *Communication Yearbook 4.* Edited by Dan Nimmo. New Brunswick, N.J.: Transaction Books, 1980, p. 179.

Burgoon, Judee K., and Saine, Thomas. *The Unspoken Dialogue: An Introduction to Nonverbal Communication.* Boston: Houghton Mifflin, 1978.

Eisenberg, Abne M., and Smith, Ralph R. *Nonverbal Communication.* Indianapolis, Ind.: Bobbs-Merrill, 1971.

Ekman, Paul, and Friesen, Wallace. *Emotion in the Human Face: Guidelines for Research and an Integration of Findings.* New York: Pergamon Press, 1972.

———. "The Repertoire of Nonverbal Behavior: Categories, Origins, Usage, and Coding." *Semiotica* 1 (1969):49–98.

———. *Unmasking the Face.* Englewood Cliffs, N.J.: Prentice-Hall, 1975.

Hall, Edward T. *Handbook for Proxemic Research.* Washington, D.C.: Society for the Anthropology of Visual Communication, 1974.

Knapp, Mark. *Nonverbal Communication in Human Interaction.* New York: Holt Rinehart and Winston, 1978.

Trager, G. L. "Paralanguage: A First Approximation." *Studies in Linguistics* 13(1958):1–12.

3
Communicating in Relationships

Thinking about Relationships

Relationships are, to say the least, complex and confounding. What is important or obvious to one person in a given relationship may not be important or obvious to the other party in the relationship. If I had a dime for each time I turned to my wife and said, "What's wrong?" Only to hear her say, "Well, if you don't know, I'm not going to tell you," I would be a very rich man. Certainly this does not mean that my relationship with my wife is a bad one; it simply points out an important element which is common in all our relationships: Things said, things done and things integral to a relationship cannot be taken for granted. Simply put: Developing relationships is hard, hard work. Feelings, desires, and expectations of each person in any given relationship are always changing and need to be addressed by the other "significant" member in the relationship.

Defining a relationship as good or bad, healthy or unhealthy, stable or unstable, is one of the most difficult tasks one can do. Coming up with a definition is a good start, but in order to have a fully satisfying relationship, we must make sure that the other party in the relationship accepts the definition. There is a good chance that the other significant person will not totally accept our definition. If this is true, one should not view the relationship as a disaster, or, if the relationship is in the initial stage, as a sign of certain demise.

Relationships are based on *compromise,* and compromise is produced by good *negotiation.* It is a myth to believe that a relationship is fifty-fifty. If this were true, then relationships would have little or no *outcome*. If one partner says, "I want to go to a movie" and the other partner says, "I don't want to go to a movie but I do want to go dancing," a fifty-fifty relationship might suggest no bending on either part so they both end up sitting at home. It is a stalemate. Neither partner gets what he wants and both may feel bitterness and anger toward the other. This is hardly a positive step toward developing a satisfying relationship. In order to have a healthy relationship, each party must feel respected as a productive member in the relationship.

Viewing Relationships in Economic Terms

In a training session which I conducted, a group of men and women were disclosing their frustration and overall discontent with their intimate relationships. Each was seriously considering exiting from their relationships but could not fully explain why. I asked each of them to get a savings passbook from their banks. I then instructed them to indicate things they did (clean, cook, buy gifts, offer strokes) for their partners in the deposit (*costs*) column, and to indicate what their partners did for them in the interest (*rewards/payoff*) column. After one week of doing this exercise, group members told me that there were many entries in the deposit column and very few to none in the interest column. This exercise helped me explain to them that relationships are based on costs and rewards—human economics.

The idea of viewing relationships in an economic way appears cold. But it is really a very helpful way to monitor a relationship. If you do not get any interest from your investment, you eventually drop the investment. In a relationship, investments are always made. Investments of time, money and energy deserve interest from the other. This does not at all suggest that a healthy relationship must be a reciprocal relationship. The group members discussed earlier were not receiving enough interest for their investments. As a result, their relationships were in trouble.

Social Exchange

A more specific discussion of relationships and economics can be seen by the theory of *social exchange* (Homans, 1961). Simply stated, exchange theory *sees the interaction between two people in a relationship as a function of what each person gets out of the relationship:* no payoff (interest) in the relationship, no relationship. This idea reinforces the "passbook" scenario and reaffirms the position that without rewards or interests, a relationship cannot exist.

Comparison Levels

Each of us compares our present relationships with past relationships, and with other available or potential relationships. After all, how else would we know if our current relationship makes us happy? The level enabling us to compare our present relationships with past relationships is called the *general comparison level*. This is the level which *measures the degree of satisfaction we feel in the current relationship*. The other level, enabling us to contrast our present relationship with the potential payoffs existing in other available relationships, is called the *comparison level of alternatives*. This is the level which *measures the degree of stability we feel in our current relationship*. These two comparison levels tend to produce four possible kinds of relationships:

1. *Satisfactory and stable:* The interest in the current relationship is greater than the general comparison level, and greater than the comparison level of alternatives.
Possible communication: "This relationship is better than any I have had in the past (general comparison level), and there is no way that anything in the future could match it" (comparison level of alternatives).
Other examples: A marriage when both partners are totally content; a person fully satisfied with his career.

2. *Satisfactory and unstable:* The interest in the current relationship is greater than the general comparison level, but less than the comparison level of alternatives.

   Possible communication: "I really like my job because it is the best I've ever had (general comparison level), but I would like to make more money and increase my chance for promotion, and I just can't do it here" (comparison level of alternatives).

   Other examples: Two friends preparing to part; changing a career.

3. *Unsatisfactory and stable:* The interest in the current relationship is less than the general comparison level, but greater than the comparison level of alternatives.

   Possible communication: "This marriage that I'm in is miserable. I really enjoyed my life before I got married (general comparison level), but if I divorce her, she'll take me for all the money I have" (comparison level of alternatives).

   Other examples: Staying in a bad marriage because of the children; not dropping out of school for fear that your parents would reject you.

4. *Unsatisfactory and unstable:* The interest in the current relationship is less than the general comparison level and less than the comparison level of alternatives.

   Possible communication: "All of the relationships I can remember have been better than the one I am in now (general comparison level), and anything I get into in the future is sure to be an improvement" (comparison level of alternatives).

   Other examples: Leaving your present job because it is the worst you ever had, and the new job offered to you is a good alternative; ending your marriage because the past was better than what you are presently experiencing, and the future can only bring something better.

Like other features in human communication, comparison levels are dynamic, on-going processes. They change over time. As an individual experiences satisfying relationships, his comparison level rises; as he experiences poor relationships, his comparison level drops. Moreover, comparison levels vary from one person to another depending on the degree to which a person feels in control of his own destiny.

Interpersonal Needs

Schutz (1958) identifies three interpersonal needs that are important to human beings. These needs are (1) *inclusion;* (2) *control;* and (3) *affection.* What is especially important is that each individual has a need to express and receive each need. The degree of expressing and receiving is, of course, dependent on the type of person, his self concept, and his general sensitivity to people around him.

Inclusion is a *person's ability to take interest in other people, and having other people interested in him*. Control is a *person's ability to respect others, and having others respect him*. Affection is a *person's ability to like or love other people, and having others like or love him*. Basically, inclusion is concerned with whether or not a relationship exists. In existing relationships, control is the area concerned with who gives orders and makes decisions for whom, whereas affection is concerned with how emotionally close or distant the relationship becomes. These needs also help one to understand his self concept. For example,

Inclusion—Is the Self	Control—Is the Self	Affection—Is the Self
Significant?	Competent?	Capable of loving?
Worthwhile?	Responsible?	Of being loved?

Good relationships make us feel good, and bad relationships make us feel bad. An understanding of our needs and how they affect our relationships is important.

Viewing Relationships

In measuring these needs, Schutz devised an instrument called *FIRO-B*, which stands for *Fundamental Interpersonal Relationship Orientation-Behavior*. It is an instrument which enables the respondent to answer questions pertaining to his or her feelings about his or her relationships. Upon completion of the inventory, the respondent secures a score, ranging from 0 to 9, on each of the needs. The numbers are fairly arbitrary, but 0 to 4 is a relatively "low need", 5 is moderate, and 6 to 9 is high. These numbers are helpful in determining strengths and limitations in a given relationship. Say, for example, you are having a problem with your boy/girlfriend. Both of you take the FIRO-B inventory and score the following:

Figure 3.1.
Potential Problem Relationship—FIRO-B

(Person A)	Inclusion	Control	Affection	(Person B)	Inclusion	Control	Affection
Express	2	9	8	Express	8	9	8
Receive	9	0	8	Receive	2	0	8

In interpreting these scores, you can see that with inclusion, both of you seem to complement each other well. With control, both of you seem to have a high need to control and very little need to be controlled. With affection, each of you have a relatively high need to express and receive affection. Can you identify a potential problem with your relationship? Both of you seem to complement each other in regards to inclusion. Both of you seem to share parallel needs in regards to affection. But control seems to be a potential problem. If both of you possess a high need to control, and a very low need to be controlled, conflict will be inevitable. Remember that compromising and negotiating are critical factors for nurturing healthy relationships and for achieving productive outcomes in a relationship.

Needs and Types of Relationships

Three types of relationships can be seen by FIRO-B scores and by other forms of communication assessments. But sometimes, active listening and common sense are all one needs to identify relationship types. These relationships are (1) *complementary;* (2) *parallel;* and (3) *symmetrical.*

If two people facilitate each other quite well, then a complementary relationship is taking place. This kind of relationship is the *most common type of relationship.* Examples might include a relationship between a doctor and patient; lawyer and client; and teacher and student. On a FIRO-B, a complementary relationship on inclusion might look like this:

Figure 3.2.
Complementary Relationship—FIRO-B

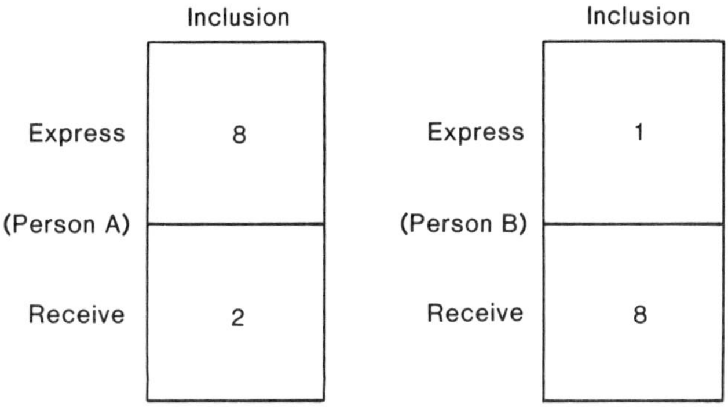

	Inclusion		Inclusion
Express	8	Express	1
(Person A)		(Person B)	
Receive	2	Receive	8

A parallel relationship is considered to be the most ideal type of relationship. It is a relationship *characterized by total trust, openness and spontaneity.* It is a peak relationship and difficult to achieve, yet it is the type of relationship worth trying to develop. On a FIRO-B, a parallel relationship on affection might look like this:

Figure 3.3.
Parallel Relationship—FIRO-B

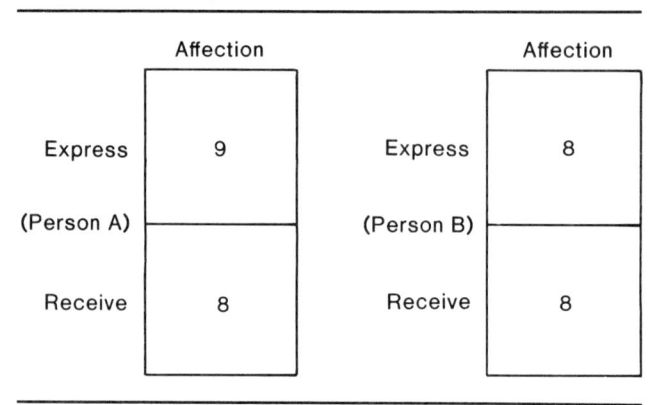

	Affection		Affection
Express	9	Express	8
(Person A)		(Person B)	
Receive	8	Receive	8

A symmetrical relationship is considered to be the most problematic type of relationship. It is the kind of *relationship that occurs when two people seem to have the identical need at the identical time.* Having a symmetrical relationship, or a symmetrical need, can cause aggressiveness, poor listening and considerable conflict. On a FIRO-B, a symmetrical relationship on control might look like this:

Figure 3.4.
Symmetrical Relationship—FIRO-B

	Control		Control
Express	9	Express	9
(Person A)		(Person B)	
Receive	1	Receive	1

This is the "problem" relationship discussed briefly in the previous section. If a couple is experiencing a symmetrical relationship or a symmetrical need, good negotiating skills are needed to minimize conflict.

It is important to note that scores on a FIRO-B, or scores on any other communication or psychological instrument, are not always entirely valid or reliable. They are simply tools that enable one to gain further understanding and insight into existing relationships.

On Being Assertive

Your grandmother wants you to come to her house every Sunday for dinner, and you feel uncomfortable telling her that coming every Sunday isn't convenient. After all, you don't want to hurt her feelings. You have been waiting over ten minutes for a parking space and when the space finally becomes available, some motorist pulls in the space instead of you. Your roommate is a slob and you don't know how to tell him that his messiness is bothering you. You have trouble asking for a raise, or feel uncomfortable going into your professor's office, or even feel shy about returning merchandise. Have you ever felt "ripped-off" by your plumber, electrician or auto repairman? If any of these situations sound familiar to you, do not be alarmed because you are not alone.

The discomfort we feel when experiencing these, or any difficult situation, stems from our inability to *assert* ourselves. Oftentimes, people confuse assertiveness with *aggressiveness,* but they are hardly the same. When one is aggressive, one is promoting conflict. The aggressor rarely gets what he wants because of the anger felt by the other. An assertive person stands up for his fundamental rights, and with cautious communication, says what he means and means what he says.

Assertiveness Is Winning Communication

Assertiveness is always a win situation. If the assertive person does not get what he wants, then at least he knows that he tried his best. This may not seem to be a great consolation, but how many times have you come home at the end of a day saying to yourself, "I wish I had another chance at that character." or "How dare she make me feel that way . . . if I only had the opportunity to deal with her again, it would be different." These typical frustrations stem from the *passive-compliant* position that we took at the time of interaction. So what will it be: aggressiveness, passiveness or assertiveness? Assertiveness seems to be the best option.

Results from Not Fighting for Your Fundamental Rights

According to Alberti and Emmond (1974), not fighting for your fundamental rights means that:
- We may end up with shoddy merchandise and service;
- We bottle up our real feelings;

- We don't do anything to improve a bad situation that already exists and needs improvement;
- We are cheating another person out of a chance to air the real issues;
- We get involved in situations we would rather not be in;
- We end up being a "yes" person—having to do all the work while others sit by and watch;
- We run into major communication barriers because no one says what he or she wants, needs or expects.

When we do not stand up for our basic rights, we end up hurting our self image. The definition that we have given to ourselves begins to change. This change affects the relationship that we have with ourselves and the relationship we have with others.

What Stops Us from Being Assertive

Sometimes, we just don't feel comfortable with the situation or the other person involved in the communication encounter. Frequently, we feel apologetic about our shyness. We allow guilt to enter our decision-making process, and as a result, we distort our feelings and desires in order to protect the other. There are other feelings which keep us from asserting ourselves. These may include (1) *laziness;* (2) *apathy;* (3) *feelings of inadequacy;* (4) *fear of being considered unworthy, unloved or unaccepted;* (5) *fear of hurting the other person or making him angry;* (6) *fear of getting no reinforcement;* (7) *fear of not knowing how to accomplish a goal; and* (8) *feeling that if we don't do it, someone else will.*

Taking Control

Regardless of the reason(s) why we have a difficult time being assertive, it is important to remember two very important steps that will help us get into the assertive *"spirit"*. The first: When we are assertive, we gain and maintain a degree of control over our lives. The second: Developing skills in assertiveness is a gradual process. We cannot change our communicative behavior overnight. We need to understand our communication styles and our communication strengths and limitations before effective assertiveness can take place.

Improving Skills in Assertiveness

The skills suggested are to be viewed as possibilities for developing an assertive style. One cannot do them all overnight. Remember: Developing assertiveness is like breaking a habit. It is a gradual process. So be patient.

- *Identify your communication strengths:* Through trial and error, we can learn ways to evaluate our behavior. We discover standards that fit our personality and lifestyle. Our judgment can be the best guide for monitoring our communicative style.

- *Use "I" statements:* Beginning your statements with "I" makes it very clear to the other person that you have feelings, needs and expectations that must be communicated. By using "I" statements, you make it clear that you are taking responsibility over your communication.
- *Don't overapologize:* Don't overapologize or overexplain. When others demand long explanations, they are manipulating our behavior and feelings. No friendship should be based on the requirement that we explain our behavior at every turn.
- *Feel free to change your mind:* Changing your mind simply means that you are monitoring your communication and wish to alter it. Don't allow people to make you feel bad for doing so.
- *Feel free to make mistakes:* Making mistakes, and learning from our mistakes, provides us with good, productive information about ourselves and others around us. Those who make us feel bad about our mistakes are the ones making the greatest mistake of all.
- *Learn to recognize unanswerable questions:* Sometimes, people ask us questions that cannot be reasonably answered. Questions like, "Why didn't you remember to. . .?", "What would this world be like if. . .?", "Didn't you know that would happen. . .?" Others may expect some profound response, but your best bet is, "I don't know. It is a question that could not possibly be answered with clarity."
- *Feel free to say, "I don't understand."* It is always important for us to seek clarification to vague communication. Increasing understanding is a critical factor in developing assertiveness.
- *Feel more comfortable about saying, "No."* Most of us don't like saying "no" because we don't like rejecting anyone. Generally this is good. Being interpersonally sensitive is an excellent human characteristic. But when we say "no" we are saying that we do not have the time necessary to do a quality job. Would you rather say "yes" and do a miserable job? If the other person understands us and knows us, he will understand when we say "no."

Improving or developing skills in assertiveness can be one of the most challenging and rewarding skills one can learn. It is important to know that like developing any skill, one must be *consistent* and *persistent* in developing skills in assertiveness. Do not give up, because assertiveness is viewed as

Positive Self-Expression = Positive Self-Respect
Producing
Productive Communication

Communication Climate

Good communication takes place if the communicators are supportive of each other. When communicators take on a defensive climate, the communication can be highly distorted and can take on an argumentative flavor.

Defensiveness can be defined as *that behavior which occurs when an individual perceives or anticipates threat.* Defensiveness is typically reciprocal. This means that if one person is defensive, there is a good chance the other will take on a defensive spirit too. Gibb (1961) has identified behaviors that can communicate either supportiveness or defensiveness:

Supportive Behaviors	Defensive Behaviors
Description: Identifying feelings, describing problems.	Judgmental: Overly evaluative.
Problem-Orientation: Looking at a problem together with no predetermined attitudes or solutions.	Controlling: Always needing to have things done your way.
Spontaneous: Being straightforward and honest.	Strategic: Manipulative and deceptive.
Emphatic: Willingness to share feelings.	Neutral: Only wanting facts; little concern with emotion.
Equal: Acknowledging both viewpoints and opinions.	Superior: Believing that your way to solve a problem is the best way.
Provisional: Knowing that there are no sure ways to deal with any problem.	Certain: Thinking that there is only one way to think of problems, issues and the like.

A *supportive* climate tends to promote better listening, more comfortable disclosure and less distortion. A *defensive* climate tends to promote conflict, poor listening and less disclosure. Doing what we can to foster supportiveness in our communication is important because

Good Climate = Good Communication
and
Good Communication = Productivity

Self-Disclosure

At times, our society makes fun of *self-disclosure*. Game shows like the "Dating Game" can make the point. In this show, a host comes out on stage and, depending on the time of the show, will introduce three bachelors or bachelorettes who are hidden offstage. At that point, the "interviewer" enters the scene, and without seeing his or her respondents, spends about seven minutes asking questions like: "What is your favorite color socks?" "If you had to choose a nickname for me, what would it be?" or "How many rooms do you have in your apartment?" These questions are innocent enough, but after a few minutes of questions and answers, the questioner chooses his or her dream date to accompany him or her to the Bahamas or St. Moritz for an extended weekend.

Once the choice has been made and the faces are disclosed, the chooser always seems pleased with the choice. On national television, one cannot say, "Gosh you're ugly. I think I'll change my mind and choose this other guy." But I know that it may be just the thought running through the person's mind. Did these game show respondents disclose information? Did they disclose enough information for the questioner so that the questioner could make a clear choice?

Based on the definition of self-disclosure, these respondents did disclose. Self-disclosure can be defined as *communicating any information which is beyond the obvious*. Disclosure, in its purest form, *is an attempt to let authenticity enter our social relationships.*

Levels of Sharing

Imagine a person as an onion conceived as a series of layers which are gradually peeled away. These can be viewed as levels of sharing, or levels of communication (Powell, 1969). The outside layer might be called *"cliche"* communication. This is the layer requiring the least amount of sharing between communicators. It is characterized by small-talk and superficial communication. Communication specialists are not sure whether we take this form of communication very seriously because if you were to say, "Good morning" to someone, and that person spent three hours telling us what a miserable morning it has been, we might think twice about saying, "Good morning" to that person again. The next layer requires a bit more sharing than did the first. This layer can be called, "factual" communication.

Factual communication suggests that we report the facts about others. We reveal very little about ourselves. Instead we tell what others have done. We even engage in gossip. The third layer can be called *"judgmental"* communication. In this stage, we begin to tell something about ourselves. If we feel the other person disapproves of our judgments and ideas, we can retreat from the encounter. It is a level that requires a greater degree of sharing.

Next, we have a level of sharing requiring even a greater degree of sharing. We can call this level *"emotional"* communication. We disclose our feelings and emotions. We tend to talk about unique things about ourselves. And the last level requires the greatest degree of sharing. This level can be called "peak" communication. *Peak* communication is characterized by total openness, spontaneity and trust. Clearly, as the levels of sharing increase, so does the disclosure. The greater the degree of self-disclosure, the greater the risk.

3.5.
of Sharing

Q: at what level of self-disclosure should corp. people function?

Emotional
"Sally, I feel comfortable with you."
"I feel the same way, Bill. I feel like we've known each other forever."

Peak
"Bill, I . . . I . . . I . . ."
"You don't have to say it, Sally, I know what you're feeling."

Cliche
"Great party isn't it?"
"Yes, I guess so."

Judgmental
"I think the band is great."
"Yeah, but they play a little too loud."

Factual
"My name is Bill, what's yours?"
"My name is Sally."

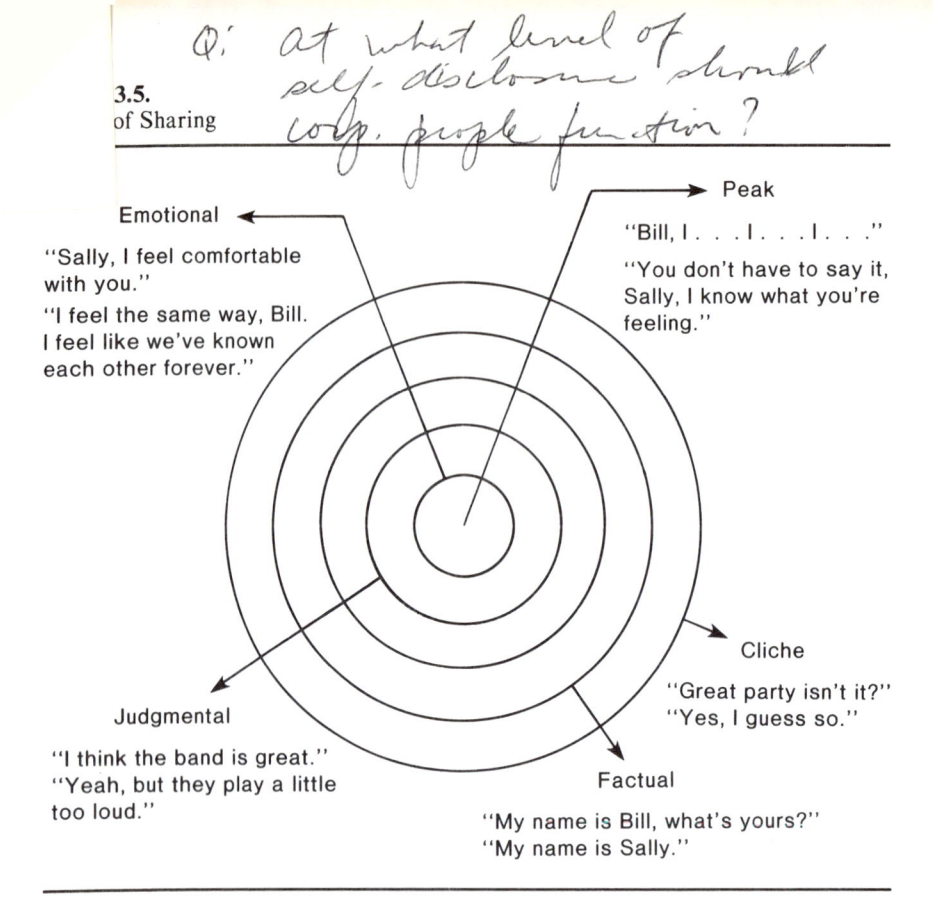

This "soap-opera" dialogue between Sally and Bill illustrates the "surface" ingredients which characterize the levels of sharing.

This "onion-skin" approach to understanding self-disclosure is not a new one. But like any communication model, it represents a dynamic process. It is not a model to live by. Don't go out with someone on a Saturday night, turn to your wristwatch and say, "Oh, oh, we've been together for two hours . . . time to move on to factual." That would be silly. It would be equally as silly to go up to someone and say, "I know you don't know me, but marry me and have my children." People do need to be gradually "peeled" away.

Self Disclosure Should Be Shared and Nurtured

Self disclosure allows us to establish more meaningful relationships with others. We tend to develop intimate relationships because we like knowing that another "special" person knows and understands us. Close, healthy relationships develop, in large part, because of the partner's ability to comfortably disclose information about his or her needs and expectations. If one partner has the inability to disclose information, then the relationship usually becomes "sick" and dies. But meaningful disclosure is not measured by the quantity of information disclosed, but rather the quality of information shared during the formation and development of the relationship. Quality disclosure is honest, spontaneous and assertive disclosure. Good disclosure can help fondle a relationship, instead of strangling a relationship.

Self disclosure is worth nurturing in our relationship for several reasons. Disclosure allows us to develop a great understanding and awareness of ourselves, can result in self development, allows us to establish intimacy on a more comfortable level, and allows us to feel more positive about ourselves and others around us.

Keeping a Secret

Most of us, at one time or another, have turned to someone and said, "Can you keep a secret?" What we do not realize at the time is that once the *secret* is disclosed, our "secret" is no longer a secret. Just as we own precious heirlooms, we own our private thoughts. We need to use discretion when deciding to disclose our private thoughts, because once we disclose them, we run the risk of feeling alienated or lonely. We feel as if our privacy were invaded. Keeping some of our thoughts private may be healthier than disclosing them. These thoughts give us our uniqueness, and our capacity to keep certain thoughts to ourselves gives us an important sense of control. When we feel in control of our disclosure, we tend to regulate our disclosure with more comfort, confidence and ease.

Summary

Developing and sustaining healthy relationships is a complex and confounding task. Negotiation and compromise are vital tools in developing lasting relationships. It helps to view human relationships as investments, which need to yield some level of interest in order to keep the relationship alive. The theory of social exchange helps one to view the economic principles in human relationships in clearer terms. When one determines the degree of satisfaction and stability inherent in his or her relationship, one typically uses comparison levels. The general comparison level measures satisfaction; the comparison level of alternatives measures stability. A healthy relationship is typically one that is satisfactory and stable.

Each person possesses needs. These needs include inclusion, control and affection. The degree in which one maintains these needs, as they pertain to his or her relational partner, can help one to identify a type of relationship experienced with a given partner. These relationship types include complementary, parallel and symmetrical types.

Assertiveness is a winning form of communication because if one does not get what one wants, at least one feels good about trying. When one does not fight for his or her fundamental rights, negative results can emerge. Improving skills in assertiveness is a gradual process. Developing assertiveness skills is important because a person dedicated to good communication should almost always say what he means, and mean what he says.

Regardless of the type of relationship, a supportive communication climate is always preferable to a defensive communication climate. Defensive communication can result in defensive listening, increased and considerable conflict.

Self disclosure is an important element in developing relationships, especially intimate relationships. Self disclosure is a reciprocal process; if handled correctly, it can enable one to gradually get to know someone.

Self disclosure allows us to strengthen our existing relationships, build new relationships and to feel better about ourselves. It is also important to know that too much disclosure can be counterproductive to building good relationships. We own our private thoughts. Therefore, discretion should be used in disclosing intimate information.

Instructional Exercises

1. Role-playing: Understanding communication climate. Simulate the following situation as a group interview.
    A. Boy or girl: Has been caught breaking and entering into a liquor store. He/she claims to have been joy-riding with friends. He/she was the only one caught. He/she is 16 years old.
    B. Mother: Overprotective, possessive.
    C. Stepfather: Very wealthy, has poor interpersonal relation with stepchild. He is resented by stepchild.
    D. Police officer: Good and experienced, yet has had bad experiences with juveniles.
    E. Social worker: Young, dynamic, inexperienced and sensitive.

The group interview takes place in a police interrogation room. Police officer should begin the role-play. After the simulation (10–15 minutes), the class should respond to the following questions.
    1. Was a defensive or supportive climate established?
    2. How did the relationship(s) of the interactants to one another have an impact on the communication?
    3. Was there any defensive listening? If so, what kind of changes might you suggest to make the communication encounter run more smoothly?

2. Role-playing: Understanding assertiveness.
Instructor: Generate case studies that characterize typical situations in which persons have a difficult time asserting themselves. Break up your class in groups of three. Ask one member to play his/her role in an aggressive manner and request that another member respond accordingly. Ask the third member to be an observer/educator. The observer will watch the role-play (for about 5 minutes), indicate to the aggressor how to change his/her behavior to assertiveness, and to try again.

The situation is repeated so that the behavioral changes can be experienced. Possible cases might include: (1) aggressor—return merchandise, aggressee—be the salesperson; (2) aggressor—complain to your "slob" roommate about his messiness, agressee—be the roommate; (3) aggressor—ask for the money you loaned to your friend, aggressee—be the friend.

3. The "I am" experience: Self-Disclosure.

   Have students list twenty "I am's" on a sheet of paper. Have them complete the stems in ways that will help them to reveal themselves to a group more effectively. When they have completed the stems, have them break up into groups of four to six. Let them talk about their experiences.

4. Reaction paper: Problems with self-disclosure.

   Have students write a brief reaction paper about the last time disclosing information seemed to hurt their relationship.

5. Thought paper: Interpersonal needs.

   Ask students: If you were a director of a crisis intervention center, and you would like to hire some qualified intervention volunteers, how would an understanding of Schutz's interpersonal needs help you to identify competent folks?

Additional Readings

Adler, Ronald B. *Confidence in Communication: A Guide to Assertive and Social Skills.* New York: Holt, Rinehart and Winston, 1977.

Allen, G., and Martin, C. G. *Intimacy.* Chicago: Cowles, 1971.

Brenton, M. *Friendship.* New York: Stein and Day, 1974.

Goffman, Erving. *The Presentation of Self in Everyday Life.* Garden City, N.Y.: Doubleday and Co., 1959.

Jourard, Sidney M. *The Transparent Self: Self-Disclosure and Well-Being.* New York: Van Nostrand Reinhold Co., 1964.

Tubbs, Stuart L., and Baird, John W. *The Open Person . . . Self-Disclosure and Personal Growth."* Columbus: Charles E. Merrill, 1976.

4
Communicating in the Interview

Interviews Are Not Simple Events

When was the last time you participated in an interview? Were you interviewing someone, or were you being interviewed? Was the interview being conducted as part of a job search, was it an evaluation of your job performance, was it an effort to discover the reasons for your resignation, or were you simply trying to gather some information about a person? What types of questions did you ask during the course of the interview? Did your questions allow the other person an opportunity to talk at great length, or was time limited? If the interviewee was too talkative, how did you curb the response? Are you sure that the questions you asked as an interviewer or the questions you answered as an interviewee were lawful? Did you feel good about the interview when it was over?

These questions should indicate that interviews are multifaceted interactions which have numerous characteristics. Just as there are different purposes for interviews, there are also different roles which participants can assume, different types of questions which constrain the interaction of interview participants, and laws governing the legality of different types of questions. This chapter will focus on conditions under which the most effective and efficient interviews are likely to occur.

The Interview: A Definition

We each participate in interviews more frequently than most of us realize. Whether you visit a professor in her office to clarify instructions for completing an assignment, discuss your on-the-job performance with a supervisor, answer a physician's questions concerning your symptoms, or simply apply for a position at your neighborhood fast-food establishment, you are participating in an interview. Not only does the interview situation span a spectrum of settings, it also occurs at all levels of the professional hierarchy. From the time you apply for your first part-time job, as a student, you can expect to participate in an interview of some type, and such interviews, which will often become increasingly structured and formal in nature, will continue throughout your professional life, regardless of your status or your achievements.

Even though people normally perceive the interview as a step in the job-hunting process, that only signifies one type of interview. Interviews may be used, in addition, to recruit, to appraise, to correct, to interrogate, to persuade, to counsel, or to solve problems. As you can see, the specific purposes for conducting interviews are infinite; however, most, if not all, of these reasons can actually be subsumed under the general purpose of information gathering or sharing. Even in the typical employment interview, for example, information is exchanged in order to provide the applicant and the organization with data which will aid in the decision-making process. In other words, an interviewer who asks an applicant during an interview "Why did you decide to seek a management position with this company?" is soliciting relevant information.

Regardless of the interview's setting or its specific purpose, all such interactions share certain common elements. More specifically, *interviews* are defined as *dyadic transactions between two parties who exchange questions and answers in order to achieve a specific purpose.* This definition implies that interview participants, either assuming the role of interviewer or of interviewee, engage in a face-to-face interaction to achieve a common goal. To the extent that this goal is accomplished, the interview has been successful. If, as a result, for example, decision-making is facilitated, the interview has served its purpose. The applicant and the organization can decide, at this point, the "goodness of fit" between them.

Dual Roles

Within the boundaries of the interview, participants will act as interviewers or as interviewees. In the most basic interviews, two people are involved. One will act as *interviewer* by controlling the interview, by setting an agenda, and by asking most of the questions. The remaining individual will act as *interviewee* by providing answers to the interviewer's questions and by soliciting any additional information which he or she may need. Although both of the participants may ask and answer questions during the course of the interaction, the two roles are, in many cases, actually noninterchangeable. The interviewer remains the interviewer, and the interviewee remains the interviewee in the interactive dynamics.

As you climb the professional or educational ladder, you can expect to encounter interviews which involve more than two people. It is not uncommon, for example, to enter an interview, as an applicant, and to discover that you are being questioned and assessed by five to seven persons, as opposed to one. Thus, this situation is one in which a group of individuals assume the role of interviewer, and the interviewee remains a single individual. To the extent that only two roles are involved although more than two people may be, the interview itself remains a dyadic interaction.

Let us call the former interview situation, the singular interviewer-singular interviewee interaction, a *duological approach,* and the latter, the multiple interviewer-singular interviewee interaction, a *polylogical approach.* You can expect to find the duological format most often in interviews for part-time or non-career type jobs. So, if you apply for a position as a busboy in a restaurant, as a sacker in your neighborhood grocery store, or as a custodian for a cleaning service, you are likely to be interviewed by a single person. At the other extreme, however, are some professional positions which regularly require that the applicant meet with a group of interviewers. It is not uncommon, for example, to encounter the polylogical interview if one is applying for a job as a college professor or as a corporate executive. Between these two extremes are many professions which actually vary in the approach they employ.

Types of Interviews

Although it is possible to distinguish many types and purposes of interviews, this chapter will focus on two basic types, which will prepare you to interact more effectively as an interviewer and as an interviewee.

The information gathering interview and the employment interview should complement one another. If you approach the former as an opportunity to gather current and personal information about jobs and careers of interest to you, to gain self-confidence, and to make professional contacts within the business community, it can become a very rewarding experience. It can also pave the way for future employment interviews. Do not underestimate the importance of either type of interview!

In spite of the fact that these two types of interviews complement one another, they are unique in at least three ways. They differ, first, in terms of purpose, and second, pressure, and, third, control. These three differences are minimal, however, in relationship to other features of these interviews.

The Information Gathering Interview

Preparing for and conducting the informational interview is actually a ten-step process, from the selection of a topic to the follow-up with a thank-you note. Each step is essential, and, followed closely, these ten steps will insure a successful interview.

1. *Select an interview topic which you will enjoy and which will benefit you.* Information about a job, a company, or a career you may wish to hold, to join, or to pursue at some time in the future should be such a topic.

2. *Do background research.* Seek out general objective information from the universty or public library, Chamber of Commerce, Department of Labor, Better Business Bureau, and prepared brochures from the company. Sources such as the *CPC Annual,* for example, are excellent sources for students who are interested in obtaining information about administrative, business, engineering, and science career options. This objective information includes facts concerning the company background, opportunities, requirements, benefits, training programs, locations, products, and services.

3. *State a specific purpose for the interview.* Having done background research, you should proceed to seek out more subjective information. Your primary concern here is to find out the interviewee's perceptions, attitudes,

satisfactions, and feelings regarding your topic. Possible specific purposes are "To gain information about the typical day for a loan officer" or "To discuss the undesirable features of selling real estate."

4. *Arrange the interview.* With your specific purpose in hand, set up the interview itself, using one of three techniques: personal referral, walk-in or phone call, or letters. Personal referrals are generally the most effective while letters alone are the least effective. The following two cases illustrate techniques for incorporating the specific purpose as part of the request for the interview. The inclusion of the specific purpose in the request insures that the person will have a clear idea of what you want.

> Case 1: Personal referral, phone call "Hello, my name is _____ . Joyce Crockett suggested that I call you. I am considering a career in banking and would be interested in any information you could share with me about a typical day for a loan officer. Could we set up a time for about 30 minutes, to talk about this?"
>
> Case 2: No personal referral, walk-in "Ms. Lewis, I'm _____ , a student at the University. I'm very interested in a career in real estate, but have not found very much specific information about it. I've read your column in the paper and I understand you've been involved in this field for some time. I would be interested in your personal perspective about the undesirable features of selling real estate. Could we arrange an appointment next week?"

5. *Formulate questions.* Develop questions which relate directly to the specific purpose. Possible questions regarding the former case would include, "What type of people do you work with?" or "How do you feel when you're at your job? Are there high times and low times?" These actual questions which you ask in the interview may take a number of forms; they may be *open/closed, primary/secondary,* or *neutral/leading.* Table 1 illustrates functions and examples of each question type. In most cases, the appropriateness of a specific type of question is a function of the interviewee's motivation to talk and time constraints. The only type of question which is never appropriate for information gathering interviews is the leading question.

6. *Arrange the questions in the most effective order.* The first questions should be fairly easy while the more controversial or difficult questions are most effective near the end.

7. *Practice the opening of the interview.* In the opening, strive to build rapport and a common field of experience. However, this small talk should not exceed the first five minutes in a 30-minute interview.

8. *Practice the closing of the interview.* Since closings can be awkward, try thanking the interviewee for his or her time, asking for final comments, and offering your hand.

TABLE 4.1
Functions and Examples of Interview Questions

Category	Function	Example
Open	Encourages the interviewee to talk and provides the interviewer an opportunity to listen and to observe; is time-consuming, but allows the interviewer an opportunity to observe the interviewee's attitudes and feelings.	"Describe your most rewarding college experience."
Closed	Allows the interviewer to control the interview; allows the interviewer to obtain large amounts of information in a short period of time.	"Are you willing to travel?"
Primary	Allows the interviewer to introduce topics.	"What college subjects did you like best?"
Secondary	Motivates the interviewee to enlarge upon an answer that appears inadequate.	"Why were these your favorite subjects?"
Neutral	Allows the interviewee to give an answer without direction.	"How do you work under pressure?"
Leading	Allows the interviewer to suggest the answer that is expected or desired.	"You work well under pressure, don't you?"

9. *Conduct the interview.* As you enter the interview situation, decide on an interviewing strategy. Either use a *funnel sequence,* in which you begin with open-ended questions, or use the *inverted funnel sequence,* in which you begin with a close-ended question and proceed to open-ended questions. Use the former sequence when your interviewee knows the subject matter and wants to talk; use the latter sequence when the interviewee is reticent.

10. *Follow up.* Always follow up the interview with a thank-you note, indicating within it information you found paticularly interesting or helpful.

The Employment Interview

The employment, or job interview, is designed to benefit the interviewer and the interviewee. To the extent that the interviewer is able to gain an accurate view of the job candidate, and the interviewee, in turn, is given an opportunity to examine the organization itself, a good match between the applicant's needs and the organization's general climate is likely to result. Not only does the interviewer have an opportunity to examine the extent to which the applicant will fit into his or her organization, the applicant, through the two-way conversation, has a chance to gain information which should help in making an organizational choice. One could safely assume, for example, that a person who prefers competitive or team sports in a social setting might also prefer a cooperative work environment. On the other hand, an individual who prefers to play alone (the lone jogger, for example) may also relish the idea of working alone and assuming total responsibility for his or her actions. For the person in the latter category, the axiom that a group of people thinking together are able to accomplish more than a number of individuals thinking separately may lack some credence. Although interviews should not be used as gauges for measuring an individual's aptitudes or abilities against the requirements of the job, they can, and should, be used to perform, in the words of J. P. Wanous, author of *Organizational Entry: Recruitment, Selection, and Socialization of Newcomers,* a "needs-climates matching function."

To insure success in selling youself as an interviewee in the employment interview, here are some tips to remember. These recommendations, which have the endorsement of many campus career placement services, are each essential.

1. *Formulate career goals.* Imagine that during the course of an employment interview, you are asked, "What are some of your long and short range goals?" Would you have to ponder indefinitely to answer this question intelligently? Since interviewers prefer interviewees who have clearly defined career goals, give this area some thought in advance.

2. *Research the job.* This is your opportunity to implement the information gathering process outlined in the preceding section. Far too many people enter the interview situation with far too little preparation. Find out as much as you can about the organization and the job beforehand through the literature and knowledgeable people.

3. *Practice the interview.* Pay a visit to the placement center on your campus and investigate its services. Many such placement services offer extensive information on interviewing, workshops on effective techniques, opportunities for role-playing, and sessions for videotaping. Take advantage of these services to practice extensively. Check your placement center for Dr. Frank Endicott's "50 Questions College Recruiters Ask College Seniors." These sample questions will become an invaluable aid in formulating answers to possible inquiries.

Be prepared to answer questions regarding your weaknesses as well as your strengths. Since interviewers are cost-oriented, anxious to avoid repercussions from unwise choices, and motivated to "weed out" candidates, negative information is often given higher significance than positive information in the employment interview. In fact, one researcher, B. M. Springbett, concluded, based on a study in 1958, that a single piece of negative information led to a 90% chance of a rejection! With such overwhelming odds, one must handle negative as well as positive questions with finesse. If, for example, your grades were poor during your freshman year, and the interviewer asks you to explain, feel free to reveal that because of your father's death that year, you were forced to assume added responsibilities which affected your grade point average. The important thing, at this point, however, is for you to transform this flaw into an asset. Proceed to explain how you matured as a result of that experience, and call the interviewer's attention to the fact that you have been on the Dean's List ever since your sophomore year. Remember: Explain your weaknesses, and transform them into strengths!

4. *Familiarize yourself with the interviewing process.* In the job interview, you can expect a three-part format: an introduction, a body, and a conclusion. During the initial stage, you can expect the interviewer to attempt to break the ice, to relax you, and to establish a pleasant atmosphere. During the second stage, which will consume the majority of the interview time, the interviewer assesses your qualifications, distinguishes you from the other job applicants, and entertains your questions. If this is the first, or screening, interview, do not ask about salary and benefits. For most professional jobs, you can expect a second on-site interview if the organization is interested. This is the time to address such matters. The final stage of the interview should be used to close and to reinforce the pleasant atmosphere.

5. *Attend to your image.* Because initial impressions are crucial in employment interviews, it is essential to be punctual and to dress appropriately. Most of us have heard this advice so often that we tend to take it for granted and to underestimate its importance. Such advice should not, however, be taken lightly because it is rooted in research. Essentially, a "primacy effect," as opposed to a recency effect, is demonstrated in which information which is gathered first has a more significant impact on the ultimate decision than that information which is gathered last. In fact, Springbett's research also indicated that the average interviewer reaches a conclusion about a job candidate after the first four minutes of a 15-minute interview!

Dressing appropriately implies that you should dress professionally, conservatively, and neatly. This is neither the time nor the occasion to be flamboyant. In addition, remember during the interview to relax, to be confident, to be yourself, to be pleasant, to speak clearly, and to maintain direct and consistent eye contact.

6. *Follow up.* Use this thank-you note as an occasion to extend your professional courtesy, to reinforce your interest in the position, and to offer any additional information about yourself.

Lawful and Unlawful Pre-Employment Inquiries

Imagine that you are being interviewed for a job, and you are asked the following five questions. Which are legal, and which are illegal?

"Do you have any handicaps?"

"Of what country are you a citizen?"

"List all organizations, clubs, societies, and lodges to which you belong."

"Have your wages ever been garnished by a credit company?"

"We would like a photograph to attach to your application since so many people are applying. Would you mind supplying us with one?"

Although the courts, the Equal Employment Opportunity Commission, and the state and local fair employment practice agencies may differ in their individual interpretations of what constitutes lawful or unlawful inquiries, all would agree that each of the preceding five questions is unlawful.

Legal restrictions exist which govern the lawfulness of inquiries regarding one's name; marital and family status; age; handicaps; sex; race or color; address or duration of residence; birthplace; military record; photographs; citizenship; ancestry or national origin; education; experience; conviction, arrest, and court record; relatives; organizational affiliations; credit rating; and references. To the extent that these restrictions are designed to protect organizations and agencies from grievances and lawsuits as well as applicants from discrimination, they are mutually beneficial.

The bottom line of this legislation is that an inquiry is acceptable only where the information is required for a bona fide occupational qualification or is dictated by national security laws. In other words, if the information is needed to determine how effectively you will perform a given job, it is considered lawful.

An excellent example of how such legislation can protect and benefit the organization itself was publicized recently on the front page of a southwestern city's daily paper. An aerobics instructor lost her teaching privileges at a fashionable health facility which caters to bankers, lawyers, accountants, and journalists who are generally 25 to 50 years old and who are earning at least $30,000 annually. Listing her height at 5-foot-6-inches and her weight at 135 pounds, she clearly violated the "ideal" weight of 123 pounds which some facilities specify for an instructor of her height. The club's aerobics coordinator indicated that the instructor was simply too heavy to sufficiently motivate the members to improve their personal appearance and fitness, thereby affecting her overall job performance. Moreover, the local chapter of the American Civil Liberties Union justified the club's policy and indicated that such clubs can argue that weight requirements form a bona fide occupational qualification just as a fashion model must be thin in order to attractively display a designer's garments.

This example clearly indicates that there are very few black-and-white inquiries. Rather, the extent to which a question is lawful or unlawful is often a gray area which is a function of the job itself.

Summary

Interviewing is indeed a multidimensional process, which occurs for many reasons, in many settings, and at many occupational levels. Whether you are conducting the interview or whether you are being interviewed, it is helpful to familiarize yourself with the process.

The most common interviews involve two people who interact in a face-to-face encounter to accomplish some objective. However, it is not uncommon in professional interviews to see interviews involving more than two people. Even though the actual number of people involved in the interview itself may vary, the roles remain the same. Regardless of the number of participants, you will always have an interviewer and an interviewee.

Interviews are designed to accomplish many goals, but two of the most common are the information gathering and the employment interviews. Even though these two interviews may be viewed as two completely separate, unrelated entities, they, ideally, should complement and enhance one another. Used properly, the information gathering interview should precede the employment interview. Even though they differ in several respects, they also bear several similarities.

Regardless of your role in the employment interview, you have an obligation to be informed concerning lawful and unlawful pre-employment inquiries. This legislation is designed to protect the job applicant and the organization. In short, know the law!

Instructional Exercises

INTERVIEW DIARY

For one week, keep a record of all interviews in which you participate. As you do so, record the date of the interview, the specific purpose of the interview, the setting for the interview, the number of people involved in the interview, and the role which you played. Which interview was the most structured and formal? Which one was the least formal in nature? Which was the most successful? Why?

INVESTIGATING YOUR INTERESTS

Choose an area which has always interested you but one which you have never really taken the time to investigate. For example, such areas as skydiving, deep-sea diving, belly-dancing, professional modeling, or creative writing might be included in this category. Conduct an information gathering interview to find out more about this topic.

Once you have completed the interview, critique it in terms of the resourcefulness of the interviewee, your ability as an interviewer, and the overall success of the interview itself. In other words, was the interviewee knowledgeable, well-informed, congenial, and attentive, or was he or she lacking in any of these qualities; were you, the interviewer, confident, well-prepared, appropriately attired, and organized, or were you lacking in any of these qualities; finally, what was your overall impression of the interview?

KNOW THE LAW

Search periodicals (newspapers, magazines, journals) for cases involving the use of Equal Employment Opportunity guidelines to resolve fair employment issues. Who were the parties involved? Who was the winner, and who was the loser in the case? Why? Was the decision surprising to you? Clip or make a copy of the article to use as a reference for class discussion.

ASSESSING APPLICATIONS

Collect job applications from five different sources (companies, agencies, organizations). Compare and contrast the applications, noting which conform to and which violate EEOC guidelines. As you examine these applications, what is the most common violation? What is the least common violation?

Additional Readings

BAS. *Information gathering interview.* Austin, Texas: The University of Texas at Austin Career Choice Center, 1981. (Handout)

1984–85 CPC Annual (3 vols.). Bethlehem, Pennsylvania: College Placement Council, 1984.

HABB. *The job interview.* Austin, Texas: The University of Texas at Austin Career Choice Center, 1981. (Handout)

Springbett, B. M. Factors affecting the final decision in the employment interview. *Canadian Journal of Psychology,* 1958, *12,* 13–22.

Stewart, C. J. *Teaching interviewing for career preparation.* Falls Church, Virginia: Speech Communication Association, 1976.

Wanous, J. P. *Organizational entry: Recruitment, selection, and socialization of newcomers.* Reading, Massachusetts: Addison-Wesley, 1980.

5
Communicating in the Group

What is a Group

Before discussing the principles of small group communication, we must consider what speech communication specialists mean by the term *group*. A *group is typically over two and fewer than fourteen people who have a common purpose or goal.* The notion of being *goal-oriented* helps to determine the difference between a group and a mob. Members in a group interact with one another to accomplish their goal and will hopefully recognize each other's existence so that they can see themselves as part of a productive communication network.

For most groups, two stages of interaction take place: 1) *initiation;* and 2) *maturation.* Initiation is the *stage of group process when members are disoriented and lack the ability to solve the problem of carrying out the meaningful actions for a given problem.* The nature of this communication is not substantive enough to allow the addressing of complex issues. The maturation stage is identified by an *emergence of interpersonal trust among group members.* Risks are taken. Negotiation skills are developed. In this stage, decision-making and problem-solving are potentially most productive.

Types of Groups

Effective group process is based on effective group discussion. The type of discussion which is held will depend on such factors as the number of group participants, the subject to be discussed, and the time allowed for the discussion. Some common discussion groups include (1) *panel discussion;* (2) *symposium; (3) round table discussion;* and (4) *progressive discussion.*

The panel discussion appears to be the most common type of group discussion. This group usually consists of four to eight participants, one of whom is designated as discussion leader. No prepared presentations are given. Participants (discussants) are expected to follow steps of reflective thinking (discussed later in this chapter) to find an answer to a complex, usually abstract question.

A symposium requires discussants either to deal with an assigned area of a discussion question or to present unique views on the issue. Within given time constraints, group participants talk about their topics, as opposed to delivering formal presentations. The round table discussion normally occurs around a conference table. This type of discussion does not warrant audience participation.

Progressive discussion involves several small groups which discuss different, yet specifically assigned topics relating to the common issue. For example, groups might be assigned to discuss such things as symptoms of a problem, causal links to a problem and background of a problem. Discussion may be assigned, may be elected by a group, or may naturally emerge through the group maturation process. Before the end of a discussion period, each leader reports the findings and decisions made by his or her group to the entire session.

Why Communicate in Small Groups

Functions

Clearly there are different types of group discussions, both in format and in practice. What is important to know is that small group communication has a functional purpose. This means that in the most part, the small group process must be goal directed. Although small group literature outlines numerous small group functions, three purposes appear clear: (1) *problem-solving and decision-making;* (2) *information sharing;* and (3) *providing mutual support for participants*.

Problem-solving and decision-making are common functions of a small group. Decision making and problem solving (discussed later in the chapter) are not the same thing, but work together to determine and implement policy. Frequently in industrial, business and educational contexts, groups are determined by decision making and problem solving networks. Sometimes these groups take the form of committees, task forces or special interest groups. But their primary goal is to reach a decision and subsequently solve a problem.

The group that is involved in information sharing is a group not qualified or authorized to make decisions, yet enjoy interacting with each other in order to fulfill more leisurely, interpersonal needs. A "rap" session taking place in your dormitory room would fall into this category. Although this group function is not overtly profit or "product" related, it is a function needed to help one develop such skills as active listening, leadership and team-building.

Providing mutual support for its participants is a group function which is, unfortunately, underrated. This is a problem because it may very well be a group with the most important function. These are groups that are selected and have an important common goal. That is, members need each other—desperately. Participants in this type of group oftentimes cannot function without each other. Alcoholics Anonymous, MADD, and drug rehabilitation programs are effective because of the common need felt by its members. They are able to relate to each other, to empathize with other's experiences, even to sense the pain felt by their peers. Encounter groups or group therapy sessions provide mutual support for each other because of the mutual disclosure emerging throughout the group process. But the most common type of group falling into this category is the family unit. Each of us belongs to a family.

From our family we expect unconditional understanding. We may not always get that understanding, but we may if we work at it rigorously. What is important to remember is that a family is a support network and that is why it (as a group) is more than capable for allowing open communication and mutual support for its members.

Advantages

The old cliché "two heads are better than one" certainly applies to small group communication. But there are many advantages worth considering when communicating in small groups.

1. Groups can assemble more resource material than any one given person.
2. Membership in a group tends to produce a higher level of interest in the successful completion of the task.
3. Groups can offer recognition of wider range of issues inherent in the topic than individuals working alone.
4. Groups tend to be more pleasant places for decision-making.
5. An expert in the discussion topic is likely to be in the group.
6. Blind spots are often corrected.
7. Groups offer more security in risk taking.
8. Groups can foster increased commitment in completing a task.
9. Groups tend to provide motivation.

As one would expect, small group advantages can be advantages only if the groups themselves are communicating effectively. But assuming that open communication is taking place, interpersonal trust has emerged, mutual disclosure is received and respected by each member, and role conflict is minimal to nonexistent, most of these advantages will be seen.

Small group research has reported on many cases where most if not all of the advantages listed allowed a group to increase productivity and, as a result, aid the organization in improving productivity. The classic case study is the Hawthorne Effect. These early group studies took place in the industrial setting of Western Electric Company in Hawthorne, Illinois. The results of the studies concluded that where people perceived themselves as members of a special group working on a special task, their morale improved and their productivity increased. The Hawthorne Effect exemplified a group working as a team.

The Group as a Team

In order for a small group to function effectively, members must consider themselves as a team. This means that each member should perceive himself and herself as being an integral part of the group-team. Team (group) members must understand the rules of the "game" (agenda, task-functions and personality differences) before they can complete their task effectively. Just as a football team must understand the rules of the game in order to play the game, so is the case of an effective small group. Once team spirit is initiated by group members, the difficult task of decision-making and problem-solving can take place.

Decision Making

Oftentimes people view *decision-making* and *problem-solving* as the same thing. They are not the same. Frequently we make decisions not to solve a problem. We can table a motion in parliamentary procedure or can decide not to ask our father for money because he is in a miserable mood. These are simple examples of decisions to evade problem-solving.

We make so many decisions each day, some trivial and some complex, that we probably could not keep track of them. It is through our decisions that we define who we are and what we are all about. Some of us are pessimists, some of us optimists. We try to narrow down the field of choice by reviewing possible solutions and alternatives. This is very difficult.

In a perfectly ordered world, it would be easy to make the right decision. Clearly this is not the case. As decision-makers, we weigh the odds, and our feelings are then going to affect our decisions whether we like it or not. But we are all inherently good decision-makers if we can view decision-making as an intuitive process.

Decision-Making and Intuition

Managers, financial experts, service professionals, students and virtually all productive persons may have access to all sorts of decision-making tools such as computers, financial instruments, research tools and the like. But without a "non-rational" knowing, "gut" feeling or *intuition,* these persons would be paralyzed in their decision-making ability. Will a stockbroker decide to sell even if the market is bad for a particular stock? Will a physician decide on surgery rather than opting for another kind of treatment for his patient? Will you drop a course after receiving only one poor grade in that course during the semester? Although one may have data, the decision is still up to the person. You must decide. Use your intuition.

Decision-making through intuitive action tends to test our human potential. Only when we come to that realization can we allow our intuition to help us out. Our intuition works like a subjective computer. Intuition is an *internal system which has correlated and associated ideas, thoughts and feelings in our minds from the time we were born.* Intuition is the tool which tells us to move, take action, decide. Once you have made a decision, don't worry whether it was the right decision.

Decision-Making Is a Risk

Decision-making is a *risk* because it is a leap into the unknown. You will always feel some trepidation. This is a very human response. But don't let the ambiguous feelings paralyze your decision-making ability. When anxiety sets in, decision-making can be distorted. This means that the potential decision-maker is more concerned with tragic consequences rather than the process by which the decision is made. As a result, the decision-maker loses perspective.

If you are totally dissatisfied with your relationship and you see no way to find satisfaction, exit from the relationship. Don't worry about the other members in the relationship breaking into your home at night and shooting you in the head six times. Or don't believe for a second that your parents will stop loving you because you made it clear that you want to pursue a career as a radio disc-jockey rather than attend Harvard Law School as your parents had planned for you. You really can talk to your professor about that poor grade he gave you on the last exam. He really won't spread ugly rumors about you to the entire faculty at school. Go ahead and ask for that raise. If you feel you deserve one, make it clear to your boss. Don't worry about being rejected. Try to understand that a good decision and your planned outcome are not necessarily the same thing.

Decisions and Outcomes

A good decision-maker is not one who necessarily makes the right decision. A person may lose a few hands at poker but will end up winning the game. Think of yourself as a baseball umpire when making a decision. When you make a decision, any decision, you get some "boos from the crowd," so to speak. You call things as you see them. In the long run, you will probably win. If you make a mistake, learn from the mistake. I know that is a cliché. But clichés are born of truths, and it is especially true in decision making. Consider the following model.

Figure 5.1.
A Way of Thinking About the Decisional Process

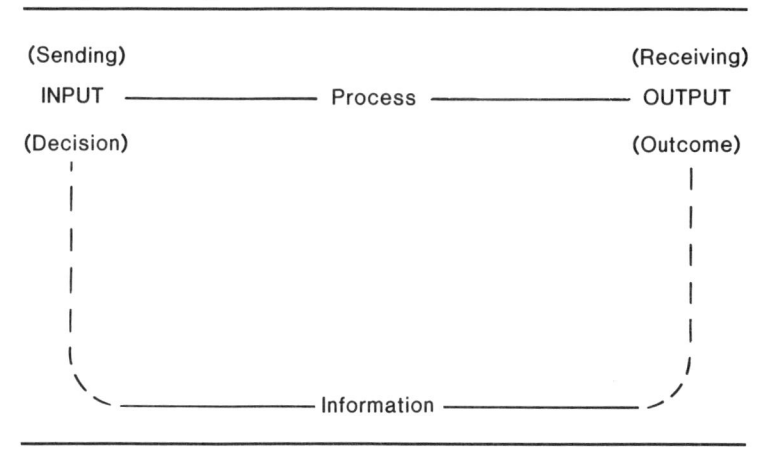

```
(Sending)                              (Receiving)
  INPUT ──────────── Process ──────────── OUTPUT
(Decision)                              (Outcome)
    │                                       │
    │                                       │
    │                                       │
    │                                       │
    │                                       │
    ╲                                      ╱
     ╲──────────── Information ──────────╱
```

Say, for instance, you are a marketing representative and you have an idea for selling a new product. You have decided to sell the product (*input*), you use a particular vehicle by which to disseminate the product (*process*), but no one is buying the product (*output*). Would you quit your job? I would certainly hope not because decisions are usually not irrevocable. The outcome tells you a great deal. Did you analyze your target audience well? Did you use an appropriate medium by which to sell the product? Did you seek enough advice before you took action? All of these questions, and many more, should feed into the (*information*) cycle. This is data which enables you to monitor your next course of action. This model can help you understand why mistakes can, at times, be constructive rather than destructive.

Another way to help us become more confident decision makers is to realize that the vast majority of our decisions are based on value judgments.

Decisions and Values

We always ased to make *value judgments*. What should I do for a living? Who will I need to lay-off at work? What kind of birthday card should I buy for Sue? These kinds of questions are difficult. Keep in mind that we are measuring values and only the individual who holds the value can make the clear decision.

What if you were in the position of having to lay-off or fire several of your employees? You must decide what is more important to you, a person who has a good track record at work but does not have the managerial skill necessary to move up in the organization, or a person who is fairly inexperienced but very motivated, or an individual who is a good, solid worker, but seems to promote conflict with everyone in the office?

It might be a good idea to generate a numerical rating system. You might need a comparison base because without one, you will have no clear way to identify a comparison base. This system will help you *legitimatize* your decision and will enable you to have a greater control over your decision. But as suggested time and time again, don't be afraid to make a decision. In the long run, a good decision-maker is a self-confident decision-maker.

Problem Solving

After one has made a decision to solve a problem, a different process emerges. There are many problem solving procedures. Some are creative. Others make use of inferential techniques, observational-deducing approaches and critical procedures. One of the best known, widely cited and more workable systems for problem solution is in the "Steps to Reflective Thinking" developed in 1910 by John Dewey. In his book entitled, *How We Think,* Dewey dissects five steps in the problem solution (reflective) process.

A Reflective Approach to Problem Solving

1. *Analyze the problem (symptoms of problem):* Something puzzling occurs in our experiences. Things are unsettled and not right. A new situation occurs for which we have no answer, or perhaps an older solution breaks down and no longer fits the needs. We have identified a problem that exists.
2. *Determine causes of problem (location):* Observations are made and data are gathered to make clear just where the difficulty lies. Where does the problem come from? What is its source?
3. *Suggestions of possible solutions (establish standards of judgment):* Potential answers explaining the problem are discussed during this step. Suggestions for discussion grow out of the careful analysis made as a result of the second step in this process.
4. *Exploration of possible solutions (weigh courses of action):* Implications of the possible solutions are probed. Consequences are investigated. A cause and effect relationship between problem and solution is formulated.
5. *Select and settle on best possible solution (consider consequences);* Here one tests by specific and planned observations the proposed solutions and their implications. Consequences of solutions are discussed.

Monitoring Problem Solving

I remember observing a group of eight men whose task it was to discuss an English curriculum in a public high school. After they discussed the issue for about thirty minutes, I noticed a great deal of frustration on their part because they were not making any progress. I said to them, "Gentlemen, you are discussing so many solutions to this problem. Is there a problem?" After about twenty seconds of silence and open jaws, they turned to each other and said, "Is there a problem? After all, we were asked to discuss it. . . . How do we know there is a problem?" After another five minutes of renovated group conversation, the members decided that a problem did not exist.

This group was given Dewey's sequence to follow while carrying on their discussion. But this group decided to deviate from the sequence. The result was an inefficient and ineffective discussion. Dewey's sequence could have guided the group toward a better, logical, clearer progression in the discussion.

Sometimes groups are given issues to discuss which are only perceived as problems by those initiating or delegating the group task. Through clear, reflective thinking, a group can tell their delegator (boss, for example) that a problem does not really exist. If all the evidence is articulated well, the boss will be thankful. This is not at all uncommon. Many managers realize their ability to exaggerate incidents and issues in their organizations, and these same managers turn to groups with the hope that those groups may help them gain perspective. This is an example of good, productive communication *monitoring.*

Just as a pilot must monitor his course of action by checking with his co-pilot and air traffic controllers, so must each group member in a problem-solving group by keeping channels of communication open. Through good, clear discussion, a group will be able to determine whether each step of Dewey's reflective process is completed.

Brainstorming

Brainstorming is an important tool used in problem-solving. As mentioned earlier in this chapter, a group can assemble more resource material than any given person. Brainstorming, and particularly creative brainstorming, is a vehicle by which group members can generate many ideas germane to an issue. Creative brainstorming should be used during step 3 of Dewey's problem solving sequence. Group members should take time to generate ideas about possible problem solutions without criticizing, expanding or developing any suggestion made. After a group has generated lots of possible solutions, discussion of each potential solution can take place.

Attitudes and the Problem Solving Group

Understanding the *attitudes* of group members, as they pertain to a given discussion topic is, to say the least, a complex task. Nevertheless, assessing individual attitudes is one of the most important things that group members can do to insure minimal group conflict. An attitude can be conceived of as a point on a continuum of response options ranging from strongly opposed to strongly in favor of. Consider the following continuum:

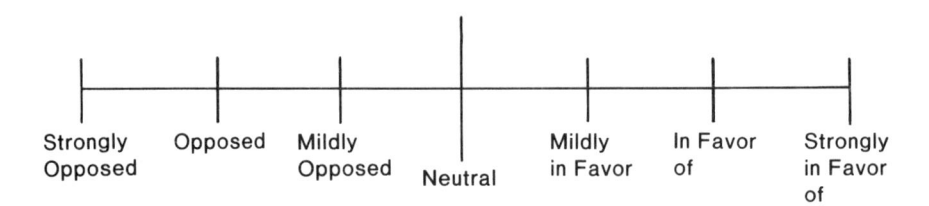

| Strongly Opposed | Opposed | Mildly Opposed | Neutral | Mildly in Favor | In Favor of | Strongly in Favor of |

If you were a discussion leader leading a discussion on pro-abortion, and your group members were all Southern Baptist women, you might expect them to place their attitudes on the issue near the left side of the continuum. You would be right to assume this placement. But this placement should provide you with vital information. Since it probably took years for your members to ascertain their attitudes, it would only make sense to assume that it would take just as long for them to change their minds enough to eventually place their attitudes on the other side of the continuum.

This means cautious discussion and sensitive leadership in leading the discussion. Everyone is entitled to his own feelings, thoughts and beliefs. But having group members place their feeling about an issue on a continuum can help make clear the possible barriers inherent in human discussion.

Latitude of Acceptance and Ego Involvement

As a discussion leader, what if you were asked to lead a discussion with your college peers on Freedom of Speech? Sounds easy enough. After all, college students are generally open-minded, and who would think that most students would be opposed to the issue.

So you begin your discussion with that assumption and ask the members how they feel about the issue. Each says, "Absolutely, I am in favor of Freedom of Speech." You think you are done. When you give your report to the rest of the class, you suggest that all of your members agreed that Freedom of Speech was great, so let's invite that representative from the Nazi party to talk to our class next month. There are screams and sneers from your group because they never agreed to such a thing. To you, however, inviting a Nazi representative qualifies as Freedom of Speech. You failed to identify the *latitude of acceptance* of the issue from your individual group members.

Everyone has a latitude of acceptance because everyone is *ego involved* with virtually every controversial issue. Identifying the latitude of acceptance of group members is a way to make an abstract, complex issue more simple and direct for

Leadership

One of the greatest myths in small group communication is that an effective group can only have one leader. This is not true. In order for a group to function well, more than one type of leader should emerge during the group process, who can influence group members in positive ways toward the achievement of their group goal.

One such member might emerge as a *task* leader, still another as a *socio-emotional* leader, and still another group participant might emerge as possessing both leadership skills. A task-oriented leader might set the discussion agenda, impose a time constraint for discussion by asking questions or making remarks. A socio-emotionally oriented leader might express a comment to a group member that would exert positive influence on the group's interaction. Or this type of leader might simply smile at a potentially threatening stage in the discussion, causing others to smile, laugh and relax. This calming period can help group participants to un-wind, and keep the group task in perspective.

Other individuals have the uncanny ability to combine task and socio-emotional leadership characteristics into their personality. The highly task-oriented leader may, for instance, carry with him or her a high level of compassion and sensitivity. Or the parent, whose overwhelming concern offer his or her child's welfare, can offer a harsh reprimand to his or her child, while following that reprimand with a gentle hug. Being stern and human are important characteristics of these (and other) examples of the well-rounded, "multidimensional" leader.

Roles

Roles are behavioral variables that affect group performance. A *role is defined as a set of behaviors which help to simplify relationships.* Remember the time you saw your elementary school teacher outside the school context? Did you run away because you felt uncomfortable about interacting with your teacher in that situation? Has anyone ever said to you, "You are not acting yourself tonight?" Many of us have been asked that question; to which we may respond, "Who, then, am I acting like?" You really are "acting like yourself." It is just that you have broken a consistency pattern for those significant others around you.

A similar problem occurs when group participants play unexpected roles in their groups. If a member has always been viewed by other members as passive or shy, and enters a discussion with aggression, this unexpected behavior might complicate the member's relationship with others, rather than to simplify the relationship with others. There are many roles that each of us play each and everyday. Getting a grip on our roles and other people's expectations of those roles is a difficult task. But when engaged in group communication three questions should be asked by you whether the questions pertain to understanding your own role behaviour, or in understanding the roles of others around you. These questions are: (1) *Is the behavior proper?* (2) *Is the behavior appropriate* and (3) *Is the behavior convincing?*

There are so many types and functions of roles integral to individuals engaged in group communications, that it would be difficult to name them all. But a partial list would include:

Examples of Roles

Goal-setter (sets agenda)	Obstructor (blocks progress)
Information-seeker (asks questions)	Synthesizer (summarizes)
Opinion-seeker (seeks opinions)	Elaborator (clarifies)
Mediator (Harmonizes)	Recorder (records group action)
Competition (tried to outdo others)	Encourager (praises other)

Clearly, some of these roles are productive roles, and some can be counterproductive to group performance. But just as each of us plays several roles (student, motorist, consumer, parent, pedestrian. . .) during the course of a day, so do group members play several roles during the course of a group discussion. As long as the multiple roles played by a member are consistent and productive, then the notion of multiple role playing can suggest a willingness to share leadership functions on the part of the member.

Role Set

The notion of *role set* helps one to understand why others may induce conflict in our lives. Sometimes we do not have total control over our roles. A role set can be defined as the *way one behaves in a role in accordance to other role behaviors interacting with his or her role.* Do you want to do one thing for a living and your parents want you to do something else? Your parents are members of your role set and their membership may be causing conflict in you.

If you were a teacher about to go on strike, you might be interested to know that you might be forced to go on strike whether you want to or not. All of the roles encircling the teacher in the following diagram make up the teacher's role set. These roles may be telling the teacher to do something that the teacher would rather not do, in this case to go on strike.

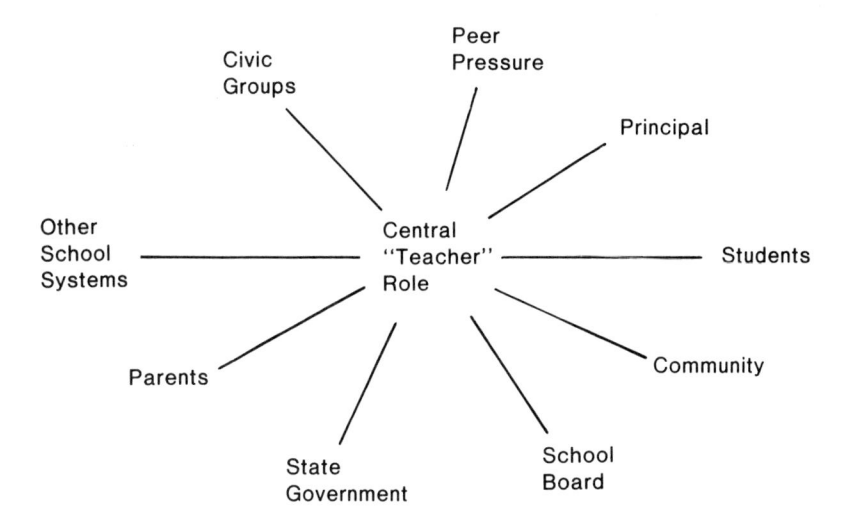

```
                    Peer
        Civic       Pressure
        Groups
                                    Principal
              \       |        /
               \      |       /
Other           \     |      /
School  ——————— Central "Teacher" Role ——————— Students
Systems         /     |      \
               /      |       \
              /       |        \
        Parents      |         Community
                      |
              State           School
              Government      Board
```

The above role set, like many role sets, may dictate the outcome of the central role. Understanding role conflict and role set can help us to identify sources of conflict or potential conflict.

Role Conflict

Role conflict is formed when there is disagreement over role perception. Two types of role conflict are especially common: 1) *intra-role conflict;* and 2) *inter-role conflict.*

Intra-role conflict can occur when there are two or more incompatible role expectations for a single role. For example: A foreman in a manufacturing plant has only one role, that of foreman. But that role of foreman may be defined differently by workers and management. Workers may expect him to represent them, and management may expect the same foreman to support and understand their contentions. Which does the foreman adhere to?

Inter-role conflict can occur when an individual is playing two roles simultaneously, and those roles are incompatible to each other. A lawyer defending his own son is playing the role of attorney and parent at the same time. Will this individual be able to do a good job? What if you were a marriage counselor and you took it upon yourself to counsel both you and your spouse? Would there be internal conflict? Inter-role conflict is very common among returning college students. A wife and mother deciding whether it is more important to do the grocery shopping or to study for an exam. How about a student's boss wanting him to work overtime when that student needs to attend an important conference with one of his professors.

Behavioral and Communication Concerns

Being aware of the nature of human behavior in a group can be one of the best ways to assess group productivity. The following chart provides a list to consider:

Necessary Behaviors for Task Functioning	Problem Behaviors for Task Functioning
Be goal-directed	Withdrawing participant
Show a sense of inquiry	Too-talkative participant
Be a good listener	Defensive participant
Be patient	Tendency to conform
Be willing to share leadership functions	Promotes conflict

This is not an exhaustive list, but the behaviors listed should give you some important things to think about. Being *goal-directed* means clarity and meaning in group discussion. Members having a *sense of inquiry* demonstrates a desire to learn and to know. *Good listening* is paramount to good communication. Good listening is active listening. Members need to minimize listening barriers and learn to interpret information accurately and to respond to information and to group members with sensitivity and thoughtfulness. Communication is a dynamic process and effective communication is frequently a gradual process. Therefore, *being patient* in a group discussion is a necessary behavior. Group members must learn to recognize their communicative strengths and limitations, and as a result, learn to identify their own *leadership style* so that they may share in leadership functions.

A group member who consistently *withdraws* from group discussion must be addressed by the group. Remember: An effective group is an effective team and a team needs every member. The *too-talkative* participant has a great deal of vocal energy, but the group must find ways to regulate that energy in a productive way. Everyone should be given a chance to participate in his own way. A too-talkative member can hinder total group participation. *Communication climate* is important to every communication encounter. For the small group discussion, supportiveness is critical for keeping conversation open and genuine. *Defensiveness* will only increase distortion and halt total group progress.

Conformity can lead to a positive group outcome. But if conformity is unnecessarily induced by members, then conformity can be counter-productive. Certainly *negotiating* and *compromising* are important and necessary group attitudes, but forcing a member or members to agree against their will can result in a disastrous group outcome. Whenever people get together, some form of interpersonal conflict is bound to emerge. But an intentional display of conflict arousing behavior from a group member must be addressed before group discussion mushrooms into an unmanageable situation.

Summary

The kinds of communicative ingredients inherent to or interpersonal encounter are also inherent to the small group encounter. The complexity of human communication, however, sometimes increases when more than two people get together in order to communicate ideas and feelings. Groups form for a number of reasons and once they form, the group process can be viewed in stages of development.

Although there are several functions for communicating in small groups, decision-making and problem-solving are the functions which require considerable skill, sensitivity and understanding. Decision-making and problem-solving are not the same. Decision-making is, in large part, a creative exercise. Effective decision-making requires one to use his or her intuition while understanding that making any decision is a risk. Good decisions and good outcomes are not always the same. Decisions are commonly value based. Decision-making is always a necessary prerequisite to problem-solving.

A good way to view problem-solving is to view it as a reflective process. There are steps that one may follow in order to thoroughly tackle a complex problem. These steps help one to monitor his or her problem-solving ability and to help monitor actions of his or her group. If one cautiously solves problems, then one is careful about dealing with attitudes, values and beliefs of individual group members. This cautious attempt to deal with group members may help reduce potential conflict.

Conflict can hurt group productivity. One of the most common causes of group conflict is conflict felt with individual roles. Everyone plays a role in group discussion, but the more simplified and meaningful one's role is, the more productive a group can be in solving problems.

Group members need to have confidence in themselves and each other. Everyone can be a leader, and everyone can be an important dimension in group discussion if they learn to develop important communication skills such as active listening, patience, and a willingness to share leadership functions.

Instructional Exercises

1. Case study: Problem-solving.

Break up the class in groups of four to six, and give them thirty minutes to discuss the following case:

The people of Nigeria are gracious and courteous in their manners. They are very generous and eager to please those whom they admire and wish to befriend. But like every culture, they have different definitions and connotations of words. For many in the Nigerian culture, the word "gift" means something different. For this group, a gift should be returned after a reasonable amount of time.

Recently, a Nigerian woman, Mrs. P., moved from her country to Los Angeles. Among her new American friends was Mrs. J. One day when visiting Mrs. P., Mrs. J. expressed great admiration over a very fine diamond necklace that Mrs. P. was wearing. Mrs. P. said at once, as was the custom of her culture, "I want you to have it by all means," and taking the necklace off her neck forced it upon Mrs. J. Mrs. J., unacquainted with the custom, accepted the "gift" and thanked Mrs. P. When the necklace was not returned, Mrs. P. explained the custom to Mrs. J. and requested the return of the bracelet.

Should Mrs. J. return the bracelet?

2. Case study: Decision-making and reflective thinking.

Have six students conduct a discussion on the following statement:

Reject, accept or modify:

"The reason that American workers are highly unproductive is because of their uncanny lack of motivation. They (U.S. workers) are inherently lazy. They don't care about the quality of their work because they have no pride in their job."

After discussion has taken place, ask the class the following questions:

1. What kind of decisions were made in the discussion, and how did those decisions affect problem-solving?
2. Was there a problem(s) to be solved? If so, was Dewey's sequence followed? If not, was Dewey's sequence followed?
3. What kind of conflict emerged from the discussion?
4. If considerable conflict emerges, how might effective group leadership be used in minimizing the conflict?

3. Small Group: Identifying leadership and communication styles.

Have the class move their desks in one large circle. Give one person a ball of string, and ask that student to begin a discussion on anything of interest to him. Whoever responds should take the ball of string, wind a small portion of it around his finger, and pass it along to the next respondent. After ten minutes of discussion, the string will illustrate communication patterns and networks. Students will be able to identify who is speaking to whom (and how often), where most of the "vocal" participation is coming from, which group members were left out of the discussion, and the like. After the illustrations have been made, ask the class to respond to the following questions.

1. Did group size affect group performance?
2. Did the string force you to conform?
3. Did shy participants feel any pressure because of the string?
4. Did the string affect the quality of information discussed within the group?

4. Attend a meeting of your city council, civic organization, or club in which you are a member. Write a description and critique of the group members and their decision-making process. How would you suggest they improve their meetings?

5. Keep a journal on discussion you have with your family. Keep running notes about their behaviors which cause conflict with other family members, their problem-solving techniques, and overall listening skills. After you have kept the journal for one month, write up a Family Assessment Report, and share your report with your family. Let them know how important they are to your life, and that the report is a way for you to apply communication principles to family communication.

Additional Readings

Bormann, Ernest G., and Bormann, Nancy C. *Effective Small Group Communication.* 3rd Edition. Minneapolis: Burgess, 1980.

Cragon, John F., and Wright, David W. *Communication in Small Group Discussions: A Case Study Approach.* St. Paul: West Publishing, 1980.

Janis, Irving L. "Groupthink." *Psychology Today* (May 1971). 5:43–46, 74–76.

Shaw, Marvin E. *Group Dynamics: The Psychology of Small Group Behavior.* 2nd Edition. New York: McGraw Hill, 1976.

Rosenfield, Lawrence B. *Now That We're All Here . . . Relations in Small Groups.* Columbus: Charles E. Merrill, 1976.

6
Communicating in the Organization

Are Organizations Important to You?

Most of you are attending college in order to achieve a primary goal: to prepare yourselves for a career in the workplace. Even though you may acquire secondary goals during your college years, such as meeting a potential husband or wife, becoming involved in campus activities, achieving recognition for academic excellence, or forming new relationships, preparing yourself for a lucrative, satisfying, and rewarding career is likely to remain your most basic goal during this important period of your life.

For this reason, very few of you will make significant changes from the career you enter once you graduate. Those who graduate and become teachers, for example, will likely remain part of the teaching profession even if you change institutions. Therefore, you would be more likely to change from teaching at the high school level to the college or university level than you would be to change from the teaching profession to the medical profession.

Because people are likely to experience life in a number of organizations over a career, it is important to examine communication-related factors which can influence one's success within any type of organization.

Whether you become a professor, a doctor, an accountant, a consultant, a stockbroker, a manager, or an attorney; whether you communicate through formal channels or through the grapevine; whether you communicate most frequently with people within your organization or with people who are outside your particular organization—there are some communication essentials which span the spectrum of organizational diversity. This chapter is designed to help you understand communication processes which characterize most organizational structures, and which, in turn, influence an organizational member's upward mobility.

Organizations: A Definition

Organizations are defined as *interdependent, coordinated units of individuals which are designed to achieve specified goals*. Organizations may, of course, be public, private, service, religious, educational, voluntary, commercial, or social in nature, just to name a few types, but these qualities are present in each type.

TABLE 6.1
Organizational Strategies

Category	Assumptions*
Rational Perspective	–Organizations exist primarily to accomplish established goals.
	–Organizations work most effectively when unpredictability in the environment and among members is controlled by rational norms.
	–Specialization allows higher levels of individual expertise and performance.
	–Authority and impersonal rules are used to coordinate and to control.
	–Organizational problems can be resolved through reorganization.
Counterrational Perspective	–The meaning of an event is determined by how people make sense of/interpret what happened.
	–Many significant organizational events and activities are ambiguous; it may be difficult to isolate the facts of the event, the reasons for the event, or the consequences of the event.
	–Ambiguity and uncertainty weaken rational approaches to analysis, problem-solving, and decision-making.
	–In the face of ambiguity and uncertainty, people utilize symbols to clarify, predict, and direct; although events themselves may be confusing, symbols make them appear logical and meaningful.

*Adapted from L. G. Bolman and T. E. Deal. *Modern approaches to understanding and managing organizations.* San Francisco: Jossey-Bass, 1984.

To the extent that the departments within an organization do operate in such a manner that activities are direct results of careful planning and coordinated efforts by management, the organization itself will be more effective. However, such a cause-effect relationship is often more ideal than realistic. What actually happens many times is that organizational members encounter certain experiences or they react in certain ways which are completely unanticipated and unplanned, and they subsequently seek to interpret these actions. Table 1 illustrates these two strategies. We will call the former strategy a *rational perspective* and the latter, a *counterrational perspective*.

Historical and Modern Approaches to Understanding Organizational Behavior

In order to more fully understand and analyze organizations, one must first recognize and acknowledge at least four different schools of organizational behavior: (1) the scientific management (classical) approach, (2) the human relations (behavioral) approach, (3) the systems (structural) approach, and (4) the symbolic approach.

The *scientific management* or classical school of organizational behavior was represented chiefly by Frederick W. Taylor, and it stressed a pro-management attitude. Workers within the organization were viewed as machines designed to produce at maximum efficiency. Workers were also assumed to be primarily motivated by monetary rewards.

In response to the first school of organizational behavior, a second one developed. As the name implies, the *human relations* or behavioral school, represented primarily by Chester I. Barnard and Elton Mayo, stressed a pro-worker attitude. This socially-oriented approach gave more attention to the workers' needs and recognized job satisfaction, social needs, and peer relationships as sources of motivation for the worker.

The *systems* or structural school of organizational behavior is a pro-organization approach which has been represented by Herbert A. Simon, Daniel Katz and Robert L. Kahn, and James G. Miller. The larger organization is the focal point, and it is literally viewed as an open system, composed of interrelated units, which interacts with and is influenced by its environment. This structurally-oriented approach recognizes the need for formal roles and relationships, rational procedures, and clearly defined objectives, to name a few.

The final approach, the *symbolic* school of organizational behavior, has emerged under the leadership of James G. March and Johan P. Olson as well as Karl E. Weick. A pro-cultural approach, this school recognizes the presence of organizational verbal, action, and material symbols, such as slogans, rites of passage, and status symbols respectively. Not only does this approach recognize these symbols as important factors which influence organizational behavior, it also accepts these mechanisms as means of describing the organization, controlling energy, and maintaining the organization.

These four approaches to organizational behavior can actually be viewed as consequential of one another, for two of the approaches are, in reality, quite mechanistic while the remaining two are quite humanistic (see table 2).

These four approaches therefore form the foundation for a study of organizational behavior and, more specifically, organizational communication.

Organizational Socialization

As you prepare to and, ultimately do, enter an organization, you will communicate with other employees (supervisors, co-workers, subordinates) during three distinct stages: pre-arrival, arrival, and post-arrival. You will ac-

TABLE 6.2
Approaches to Organizational Behavior

Category	Description
Scientific Management Approach	Mechanistic: Emphasizes efficiency—relationship between organizational profits and employee productivity.
Human Relations Approach	Humanistic: Emphasizes interdependency—"goodness-of-fit" between organizational goals and employee needs, skills, and values.
Systems Approach	Mechanistic: Emphasizes rationality—"goodness-of-fit" between organizational goals and environmental demands.
Symbolic Approach	Humanistic: Emphasizes meanings and counterrationality—"loose" coupling between organizational goals and employee behavior.

tually experience these phases regardless of the type of organization you join. In fact, even as a student, you are being "socialized" into an organization, the college or university in which you are enrolled. During this process, you actually "learn the ropes" by communicating with others. In essence, the process of *socialization* becomes *an ongoing experience during which you learn the attitudes, values, norms, and priorities of the organization and work group which you are joining.*

Think back to the period just prior to your enrollment as a college student. What were your feelings and expectations regarding the college experience? How did you formulate these impressions? With whom did you communicate to gather the information you needed? The impressions which you formed before enrolling, based on conversations with friends, conferences with academic advisors, discussions with campus recruiters, visits to the campus, and correspondence, comprised the *pre-arrival* or "anticipatory socialization" phase.

The extent to which your pre-entry expectations of the first phase were accurate was revealed during the *arrival* or "encounter" phase. Once you began to attend university classes, were your pre-entry expectations confirmed or contradicted? Were you pleased that the facilities, classes, professors, and policies were everything you expected, or were you disappointed with your findings?

Now that you have been in college for awhile, how have you accommodated this environment? It is during this *post-arrival* or "metamorphosis" phase that the organizational member begins to modify his or her attitudes and behaviors in an effort to gain acceptance. Based on feedback which you have received from professors and peers during your college experience, have you changed in any way? At the advice of your professor, did you try to develop better study habits, or did you seek out tutoring for your chemistry, engineering, or mathematics class? Did your friends persuade you to relax by joining a fraternity or by partying more? These are indeed examples of organizational communication, a process which occurs throughout an individual's career in all types of organizations—educational, business, or otherwise.

Organizational Communication: A Definition

Organizational communication refes to *all information exchanges which occur within and between formal organizations*. Even though the area of organizational communication has traditionally focused on person-to-person, or interpersonal, interactions, such as those between supervisors and subordinates or between co-workers, it is possible to extend this traditional perspective. So, no longer does it simply include the exchange of explicit verbal messages in interpersonal interactions within the organization; it also encompasses the transmission of implicit symbolic messages to organizational members as well as to other organizations. This expanded perspective recognizes the existence, importance, and functions, for example, of company logos and myths as well as the roles of instructions or orders from a supervisor to a worker. These things, and more, constitute organizational communication.

The remainder of this chapter will therefore focus on the following four topics: (1) communication flow within organizations, (2) symbolic communication within organizations, (3) barriers to effective organizational communication, and (4) techniques for improving organizational communication.

Communication Flow within Organizations

Due to the complex nature and the diverse purposes of most modern-day organizations, communication within the boundary of the organization may flow in varying directions. Communication, for example, may be formal or informal. Formal organizational communication, specifically, may be (1) upward, (2) downward, or (3) lateral in its flow, while informal organizational communication tends to be more random, and less predictable, in its flow. Both formal and informal organizational communication include serial transmissions.

Formal Organizational Communication

Formal organizational communication occurs within the framework of the organization as managers and subordinates interact with each other and with environmental forces in order to accomplish various tasks. The relationships between personnel within a given organization can be represented visually by the organization chart (see figure 1). Thus, a manager in one department who communicates with a manager in another department in order to complete a project is engaging in formal organizational communication.

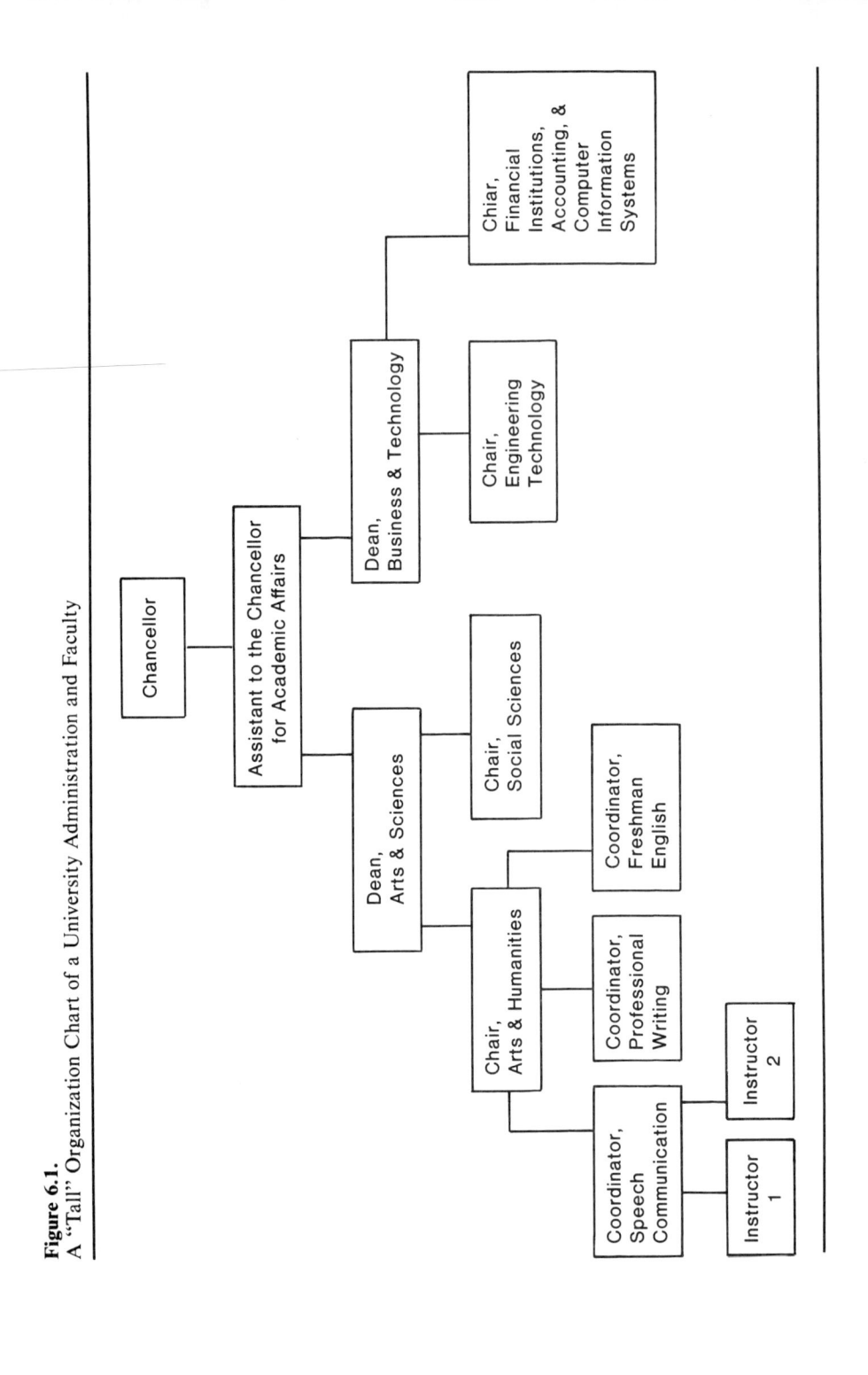

Figure 6.1.
A "Tall" Organization Chart of a University Administration and Faculty

Upward organizational communication occurs when a subordinate shares information with his or her supervisor. Such communication involves sending upward to a manager a message which may or may not concern the task(s) at hand. More specifically, upward organizational communication occurs whether the worker conveys to a supervisor personal information, information about co-workers' problems, information about company policies and procedures, or information about means for taking care of problems.

Downward organizational communication, on the other hand, occurs when a supervisor shares information with his or her subordinate(s). Such information may actually take a number of forms. Managers may provide job instructions to their workers; they may explain to their workers the relationship of one department's responsibilities to the tasks of another department; they may explain organizational policies and procedures; they may provide feedback to workers during performance appraisals; or they may attempt to inspire their workers to be more dedicated workers. All these exemplify downward organizational communication.

Whereas supervisors converse with subordinates, and vice versa, in the latter types of formal organizational communication, workers communicate with their peers in *lateral organizational communication.* More specifically, managers communicate with other managers at the same level (lower, middle, upper) to coordinate, for example, the activities of their departments.

Even though upward, downward, and lateral organizational communication differ in the direction of their information flows, they share a common element: they each characterize communication patterns within the formal organizational structure.

Informal Organizational Communication

Informal organizational communication occurs in addition to, not instead of, its formal counterpart. Rather than occurring as a result of relationships on the organizational chart, this type of communication is a function of personal relationships among organizational members. These relationships, therefore, transcend the limitations of the formal organizational structure, and they allow members, regardless of their status, who are bound by common interests, values, or concerns, to communicate.

Informal organizational communication travels through what is commonly known as a *grapevine*. The distribution of information through this network is not as rigid as the dissemination of information through formal channels. However, it is possible to observe varying patterns of grapevines which exist in organizations. For example, in one case, Jerry, the originator of the message, tells Joe, who tells Janice, who, in turn, tells Joyce, who ultimately tells Julie. In another case, Mary, the originator of the message, tells Michael, Michelle, Mona, and Minnie the information. In the former pattern, a *serial transmission* occurs because information is literally passed from one organizational member through a series of other organizational members. To the extent that such information becomes one person's interpretation of another's message, distortion is more likely to occur. In other words, the message recipients, who are involved in serial transmissions, are likely to omit, add, or alter the message details such that the final recipient receives a different version from the original message. Thus, the informal organizational communication network usually operates quickly, but the information which is conveyed is frequently inaccurate.

One final note regarding serial transmissions: they can occur within informal or formal organizational structures. Informally, rumors can circulate among employees at the same or differing organizational levels; formally, orders may be passed downward from executives through middle management to lower management. In general, however, one can expect less distortion through formal channels (supervisors, official memos, in-house newspapers, bulletin boards) than through informal networks (grapevine).

Symbolic Communication within Organizations

Although a treatment of symbolic communication within the organizational structure does not limit itself to verbal interactions, it nevertheless qualifies as a type of organizational communication, given the definition provided earlier in this chapter. Such communicative symbolism may indeed be verbally, action, or materially-oriented.

Verbal symbolic communication includes myths, stories, slogans, rumors, or jokes which tend to document and assign importance to various organizational events or people. The slogan from the local telephone company or from the well-known hamburger franchise, the rumors about that accounting professor, the stories about what happened at the company party last year—these reflect much about the life of the organization to insiders as well as outsiders.

Action symbolic communication includes rites of passage, parties, orientation sessions, and lunch breaks. The common expectation by older, more experienced employees that a newcomer, however bright, must "pay his dues" by performing certain mundane tasks, illustrates this mode of communication.

Finally, status symbols, logos, awards, and company badges illustrate *material symbolic communication.* The expectation that a company executive will drive a Mercedes Benz or the assignment of a spacious office with a "view" to a manager on the fast-track—these illustrate this last type of symbolic communication.

Although symbolic communication represents only a small segment of organizational communication, it, at the same time, signifies an area which reflects the underlying values of an organization. For that reason alone, it merits consideration.

Barriers to Effective Organizational Communication

As organizational members attempt to communicate either with their co-workers or with people outside the organization, communication breakdowns can occur very quickly. With an ever-present need for complex as well as simplistic information, managers must constantly be aware of and sensitive to potential communication pitfalls.

One communication barrier is *physical* in nature, and it includes actual message interference. Physical barriers can be visual as well as aural in nature. For example, if a worker is sitting in her supervisor's office, receiving instructions for a project, and the hum of the air conditioning unit and the sight of a roach running across the floor, distracts her, these physical noises have competed for her attention. Whenever an organizational member fails to adjust to or creates such communication distractions, barriers are erected. People's voices, footsteps, passing cars—all these represent common environmental barriers which fit into this category and which may interfere with the flow of communication.

Another type of communication barrier is *physiological* in nature. Relating to an individual's health, physiological barriers can include cramps, pain, headaches, or other discomforts. If, for example, a manager is explaining to his secretary how he wants a document typed, and the secretary has a severe migraine headache, a physiological barrier has been erected.

A third type of communication barrier is *psychological.* When a worker just does not "feel" like listening, when a worker pretends to listen to a supervisor while thinking of something else, when a worker allows personal prejudices to affect her level of attention, when a worker disregards a co-worker's comments because he dislikes her—these represent such attitudinal barriers. These problems often emerge as a result of negative or uncertain attitudes about the value of a message, the source of a message, or the receiver of a message.

A final type of communication barrier is *semantic* in nature. As our country becomes more and more of a cultural melting pot, such barriers are likely to emerge. The supervisor who says to the new clerk in his department, who happens to be from Taiwan, "That's a b-a-d shirt you're wearing", is likely to erect a semantic barrier. Intending the remark as a compliment (connotative meaning), the supervisor may be unaware of the fact that the clerk is perceiving "bad" as a criticism (denotative meaning).

Because each of these four barriers can cause serious problems and distortions in formal as well as informal organizational communication, effective intra- and inter-organizational communication is an ongoing goal in most companies.

Techniques for Improving Organizational Communication

Although the communication situation is never completely free of barriers, here are ten commandments for communicating more effectively within the organization.

1. Eliminate all visual and/or aural distractions.
2. Prepare yourself physiologically to communicate and to listen.
3. Prepare yourself psychologically to communicate and to listen.
4. Be approachable communicatively.
5. Speak clearly and distinctly.
6. Use jargon only when appropriate.
7. Use formal "standard" English.
8. Listen, initially, to understand, not to evaluate.
9. Interpret the nonverbal as well as the verbal messages of your work group and/or organization.
10. Attend to the relationship-oriented, as well as the task-oriented, needs of individuals in your work group and/or organization.

A close examination of these ten commandments reveals a type of hierarchy. To communicate effectively in any interaction—in a dyad, in a small group, or in a business presentation—it is helpful to follow these steps. More specifically, one should begin by attempting to rid the setting of any "noise" which is or which might be competitive for one's attention. If the lighting is poor, or if construction noise exists, one should make an effort to schedule a business presentation, for example, in another room.

Next, prepare yourself physically and mentally to communicate in the organizational setting. You cannot communicate effectively in any type of interaction if you are physically tired and mentally aloof. Rest adequately, and assume a positive attitude!

Now that you have prepared the setting and yourself, physiologically and psychologically, you are ready to actually engage some form of oral organizational communication. In addition to speaking distinctly and appropriately, in a manner which is understandable to all organizational members, make sure that you exhibit positive listening habits.

Finally, be aware that you, as well as the organization itself, communicate nonverbally and verbally. In fact, nonverbal messages are frequently more powerful and more believable than verbal messages, especially when the two types contradict. If you are truly as concerned with getting along with your workers as you are with getting the job done, be sure to convey it through your communicative style as well as through rewards. Let the people in your organization know that you really do care about them as well as their performance.

Summary

Just as various types of organizations have different purposes, organizations differ in how they function internally. Although organizations are often assumed to be very rational, orderly entities, they do not always operate in that matter. In reality, organizational behavior can be studied from counter-rational as well as rational perspectives.

In order to truly understand organizational behavior, one must recognize four different schools of thought concerning such behavior: the scientific management school, which represents a pro-management attitude; the human relations school, which represents a pro-worker attitude; the systems school, which represents a pro-organization attitude; and the symbolic school, which represents a pro-cultural attitude.

Regardless of the organization's type, purpose, or method of operating, however, an individual who is joining it can expect to experience a period of initiation or socialization. This socialization actually begins before the individual even enters the organization, and it continues throughout the person's stay in that setting.

The process of organizational communication itself occurs throughout this socialization period. One communicates with the organization and its members before entry, and this communication continues in the workplace throughout one's career. Not only are there formal channels of communication within the organizational structure, there are informal channels as well. In other words, one is able to share information with supervisors, co-workers, and subordinates in formalized interactions as well as through the grapevine. Both formal and informal channels of communication have their place within the organizational structure, provided the information is accurate.

Not only does organizational communication occur at a verbal level, it occurs at a symbolic level as well. Organizations and their members send signals to other organizations and to other members about values, expectations, and attitudes. Not only are these signals verbal in nature, they are also reflected through actions and through materialistic symbols.

Although effective organizational communication may be impeded for a number of reasons, there are some very good techniques for enhancing such communication. In order to communicate most effectively within the organizational setting, one must begin by eliminating barriers at an intrapersonal level and then progress to utilizing effective strategies on the interpersonal, small group, and public speaking levels.

Instructional Exercises

ORGANIZATIONAL AUDIT

Think about all organizations in which you have worked or participated in the past five years. As you think, select one with which you became unhappy, frustrated, or disenchanted, and, as a result, left. List as many reasons as possible to suggest why you departed. Did you feel as though you, as an employee/member, were treated as a person with needs or were you simply viewed as a cog in a wheel? Did the priorities of the organization itself appear to be pro-management, pro-worker, pro-organization, or pro-cultural in nature? Which of the preceding four approaches to organizational behavior do you believe is/are most sensitive to the needs of organizational members?

CHARTING YOUR COURSE

As a member of some work or social organization, you are in the process of being socialized. Select an organization to which you currently belong. At what stage in the socialization process are you right now? Are you still forming impressions based on information from others; are you in the process of finding out things about the organization firsthand; or are you in the process of changing your actions and behavior in order to achieve acceptance from others? List as many reasons as you can think of to support your choice.

COMMUNICATION ANALYSIS

When you are at work, do you talk most often with your supervisors, with your co-workers, or with people you supervise? Why? Who talks most with you in the work setting: your superiors, your peers, or your subordinates? Why? With whom would you like to communicate most often? Do you think that the quality of your job performance is influenced by the extent to which you obtain information through the grapevine?

STATUS, SIGNS, AND SYMBOLS

Since much of the communication which occurs in the organizational setting involves implicit information regarding values and priorities as well as explicit instructions and orders, one must be sensitive to all types of messages, nonverbal and verbal alike. Select an organization to which you belong, and list items which represent status symbols in that context. Are these obvious items like cars, clothes, office location, and desk size, or are they more subtle in nature? How did you find out that these things were important to your organization? Did someone tell you directly, or was it simply an observation on your part? What do these status symbols reflect about the organization itself?

Additional Readings

Barker, L. L. *Communication* (3rd Ed.). Englewood Cliffs, New Jersey: Prentice Hall, 1984.

Bolman, L. G. and Deal, T. E. *Modern approaches to understanding and managing organizations.* San Francisco: Jossey-Bass, 1984.

Certo, S. C. *Principles of modern management: Functions and systems.* Dubuque, Iowa: Wm. C. Brown Company Publishers, 1980.

Dandridge, T. C., Mitroff, I., and Joyce, W. F. Organizational symbolism: A topic to expand organizational analysis. *Academy of Management Review,* 1980, 5, 77–82.

DeVito, J. A. *Human communication: The basic course* (3rd Ed.). New York: Harper & Row, 1985.

Ferguson, S. and Ferguson, S. D. *Intercom: Readings in organizational communication.* Rochelle Park, New Jersey: Hayden, 1980.

Jablin, F. M. Organizational communication: An assimilation approach. In M. E. Roloff and C. R. Berger (Eds.) *Social cognition and communication.* Beverly Hills, California: Sage, 1982.

Southern Speech Communication Journal, 1985, 50, 189–304.

7
Communicating to the Public

You are in front of a group. Your mouth is quite dry. Your knees are trembling. Suddenly, it hits you that the time has come at last. You have to speak. You have ceased to be just another person; you have become a PUBLIC SPEAKER.

Not all suffer such obvious symptoms, but most of us do feel uneasy when we have to stand before a group, of any size, and speak. We try breathing deeply. Then we try going over our notes. Then we try imagining the audience in their underwear—an old remedy for stage fright. Nothing works! How do politicians, teachers, college professors, ministers, business leaders, club presidents, and others manage to speak before all types and sizes of audiences and not faint, or fall down from weak knees? What do they have that you haven't? Experience.

Speakers are made, not born. The college student of today is seeking more than just information about speakers. Students are seeking ways to accomplish specific goals. Public speaking is just one of the many skills needed to accomplish some life and career goals. Try to think of a successful person that you admire. Does that person spend some amount of time speaking to groups? We have to admit that even though public speaking might not be *required* for a future job, individual goals and commitments will likely require that we be able to speak before a group sometime in the future.

Every speaker is different, of course, but there are some skills that each speaker has in common with other good speakers. Think about the last good speech you heard. The speaker had good language skills. The words he chose were appropriate, vivid, and clear, and his language structure was developed in such a way that it was easy to understand what was being said. The speaker had analyzed his audience well enough to speak to the needs of that particular audience. The organization of the speech was easy to follow and remember. The speaker had chosen a practical organizational pattern to fit the subject and the audience. Last, but not least, the speaker delivered the speech with energy, animation, and expressiveness.

Each of the following topics will be covered in this order: audience analysis, adjusting topics for audiences and speaker purpose, organization, language and language use, and delivery.

Audience Analysis

In order to be a "public speaker" you have to have a key ingredient: an audience—your "public." In a classroom situation your audience is rather stable. In a short time you can know a great deal about that audience: their interests, their age range, their career goals. If you begin listening to class discussion, you will soon know some of the various emotional inclinations of the class as well. All of this information you can process and organize as you prepare to give a speech to the class.

In the socio-economic world in which you either currently exist, or will exist after you finish college, audiences might not be so easy to "read," or get to know ahead of the speech. In "real life" you are asked to give a speech because you have some information that the audience wants or needs; you are required to give a speech because your work supervision feels you have the knowledge of the topic and the skill to give it; you have achieved personal success and credibility that caused someone to choose you as the speaker for a particular event, for a particular topic, or for a particular audience. Although the audience might know something about you ahead of time, you still must make an effort to learn about the audience, if you wish to be effective.

The first question to ask is *"who"* is the audience? There could be several answers to this question that would give clues to the appropriate approach to take. Who is the audience? The answer could be the Rotary Club; or the Tuesday luncheon Rotary Club; or the suburban Rotary Club; or the annual awards dinner for the Downtown Rotary Club and guests. Each answer tells you something a little different about the group.

A second question to ask *"Is the audience all male, all female, or mixed?"* You cannot rely on the title of a group to ensure that you know the gender of the audience. An example would be going to a meeting of the League of Women Voters fully expecting all women, only to find a third to one half the audience is male.

The third question is *"What is the age range of the audience?"* An audience of retired persons, aged 55 and above, would have different concerns than an audience of parents, aged 25 to 45.

The fourth question to ask is *"What is the educational background of the audience?"* This might be difficult to answer for some groups, but it is better to know if there is a common factor in education, or if the backgrounds are mixed.

A fifth question to ask is *"Are there shared professional interests within the audience?"* Is the audience a diverse professional group, or is there a common career or related careers? Since most people spend the majority of their lives at their work, relating a topic and information to careers builds a bridge between the speaker and the audience.

A sixth question could be *"What is the occasion that brings this audience together at this time?"* A special occasion could mean a more festive atmosphere. Even if you have been assigned a topic in advance, the audience is more drawn to your speech if you make reference to the occasion or tie the occasion into the topic.

All of these questions and any others that you feel are relevant to your topic or would help you find *"common ground"* with the audience. Common ground is any shared experience, belief or emotion. The religion or religious tone of an audience might have a direct influence on the way you approach your subject and your audience. Political affiliation is another strong factor that might be considered in the evaluation of an audience. Any shared factor within the audience should be sought out and evaluated in light of its influence on the reception and perception of you, the speaker, and the speech you will give.

Physical Factors

So far we've asked specific questions about the audience and the commonalities that will make them have certain biases and background knowledge before you speak. An audience exists as a group in a place. There are some questions about the gathering of the audience that will help you evaluate them.

Where will the speech be given? Will the audience be in a room far larger than the space required for their number, or will the audience be crowded into a space too small? Will they be seated at tables with the remains of a meal still before them? It is much harder to arouse an audience spread over a space far too large for it, than if they were in a space the proper size. Tension and feelings, however, are heightened if an audience is crowded into a space far too small for it. Politicians often arrange for too small a space for the expected crowd because it heightens the tension level and it is easier to get the excited response from them that is needed to get good media coverage and generate more enthusiasm among followers. One of the most difficult situations in which to speak is just following a meal, especially if the audience still has the remains of the meal before them. The speaker must be aware of keeping the attention of the audience. "After Dinner Speakers" often rely on humor, high interest stories, anecdotes and other devices to keep the interest of the audience.

When will the speech be given? Will you follow other speeches? Will you follow a lunch or a dinner? Audiences become more tired, less attentive as the night wears on. If you know in advance that your speech will *follow* other speakers or a lunch or dinner, you can plan to include material that will help keep their attention. If the speech is late in the evening, you could use this as a reference point for the audience, keeping them alert to the time you use in the speech.

Will you be facing an audience auditorium style, or will they be seated around you? Is there a possibility of part of the audience having to stand during the speech? A good speaker tries to get eye contact with the audience. Knowing ahead of time the configuration of the audience will help you plan how to get good eye contact with members of the audience. If there is a possibility that some or all of the audience will be standing, you have an obligation to use the time very wisely. Only a few speakers are so good that they can keep a standing audience's attention for long periods. Although the speaking time may pass quickly for you, it may seem quite long for someone standing.

Will there be a microphone? Should you use one if one is available? Depending on the size of the audience and the structure of the room and any outside noises, you may decide a microphone would help the speaking situation. Plan ahead for such a decision. You will probably have to ask for amplifications if it is not offered. Just a word of warning: Just as it would be difficult for an audience of three hundred to listen to you in a noisy open auditorium with no amplification, it would be just as distracting to boom through a microphone at a group of twenty. Judgement should be exercised in deciding to use a microphone.

Most of the questions you could ask about an audience and a speaking event should be done well ahead of the speech. During the speech there are questions you should ask yourself.

Can they hear me? A sure way to determine if you are being heard is to check out the back row. Are they leaning forward more than other members of the audience? Are they looking about or seem disinterested? Rather than asking if you can be heard, you might want to raise the volume of your voice first to see if they lean back in their seats, or if you get their attention.

Are you keeping their interest? Shuffling, fidgeting, coughing, rustling papers are all signs of lost interest. You might be able to mentally take notice and make some quick changes in your speech. You might realize that you gone too long for the audience. As a college professor who speaks before an "audience" almost everyday, I can tell when it is time for class to be over without consulting a watch: books close, notebooks rustle, and students begin to lean toward the door, even the most interested, motivated students. I quickly take the hint and come to a close.

Has some event, disaster, sudden change affected this audience? Are you having to speak just after they put out a fire in the rear of the auditorium? Lots of things can happen to an audience. It is better not to ignore that event. I can think of two examples of how acknowledging an event or ignoring it can make a difference. At the 1977 Florida Speech Communication Association Convention in Orlando, the first speaker at a morning meeting was to be Theodore Clevenger, Jr., Dean of the College of Communication at Florida State University. The audience was buzzing that morning because the news had come that the famous entertainer Bing Crosby had died. Dean Clevenger, being a capable speaker, quickly reorganized his speech to include comments about the passing of this famous singer-actor. The immediacy of our experience assisted in strengthening the impact of the speech. On the other hand, I was part of a church service, when at the very opening it was announced that a very well-known and well-loved lady had had a sudden stroke and died that morning. I, along with others, was shocked by the news. Not another mention was made of the event. Few in the audience kept attention to the sermon that day. These two contrasting examples show us that we as speakers must be alert to the audience as persons.

Adjusting Topics to Purpose and Audience

You may have realized by now that not all audiences will respond to the same general topic in the same way. You may think of yourself as something of an authority on cars, all kinds of cars. You may even feel that you are something of an expert on the general topic of cars. Indeed, a number of groups in your community are interested in hearing a speech on the general topic "cars." The local Parent/Teachers Association wants to hear a speech on new car safety devices for children. The Mothers Against Drunk Driving wants to hear about the progress of a law restricting the sale of cars to multiple DWI offenders. The local Association of Taxpayers want to hear some suggestions for keeping down the cost of car tags. The Auto Body Class at the local technical college wants a speech on new types of polymer auto paints.

What is the basic differential among all of those "car" speeches? First, you noticed that beyond the general topic, the specific topics are all different. There is a big difference between "New Car Safety Devices for Children" and "New Polymer Paints for Long-Lasting Car Finishes." The specific topics are quite different, but their general purpose is the same. Each speech is supposed to present some information to the audience. The general purpose of each speech is to inform. In fact, we call this type the Informative Speech.

You are now wondering about that speech on the progress of a law to restrict the sale of cars to multiple DWI offenders. Indeed, it could be an informative speech, if the speaker only told the particular facts about the formation of the law and the impact it might have if passed. The speaker might want to get the audience to do something to influence its swift passage in the Legislature. The speaker would then outline a course of action the audience could follow in order to get the bill passed more quickly. The speaker would want to motivate the audience to carry out a plan of action to the end of getting the law implemented. The specific topic of the speech then would be "Getting the DWI Car Purchase Law Passed." The general purpose of the speech is really to persuade the audience that the law is needed and what to do to get it passed. This type of speech is called the Persuasive Speech.

On any speech occasion the speaker must not only choose a topic, unless it has been chosen already, but the speaker must also determine the *purpose* of the speech. Whether the speech is to be *informative* or *persuasive* will determine the organizational pattern and the language to be used. Along with the information you've gathered through your audience analysis, you can begin to collect and organize the data to build the speech.

Although the informative and the persuasive speech are the two most basic types, some speeches are labelled the "Speech to Entertain." This type is most often found in an after dinner situation, when no particular topic is called for. However, the speech whose purpose is to only entertain is not to be found as often as it once was. Audiences today consider their time to be of value to the point that a speaker has to have a well delineated purpose. That does not rule out the fact that a speech should not be entertaining. You may wonder how you can do well if you have to inform or persuade and entertain at the same time. You might even think "How can I think of that many jokes and fun stuff every time I give a speech?" Let's adjust our thinking about the word "entertain." When you say "I entertained guests at my house," you are not saying that you joked with them or had a great time. What you are saying is that you brought some guests into your home. You let them in and included them in your meal or your evening conversation. Think of entertaining as "bringing in" or including. You want to bring the audience into your speech so that they will stay with you, or think in the direction you want. Every good speech has a quality of entertainment.

Data Gathering and Organization

Many speech teachers have been asked by students preparing to give their first speech "How do I start? Where do I get stuff about my topic?" Stuff is right! The "stuff" that of a speech is data. *Data is any material used to formulate the speech.* Data can be statistics, testimony, stories, anecdotes, examples, illustrations, usual aids. The obvious place at a college to collect data is the library. Besides a library, there are all sorts of sources for data, such as interviews with experts, radio, television, records, videos, letters, memos, pamphlets, diaries, and any other viable source.

Whatever the source, the speechmaker must be sure that source is the best available and that accurate and complete notes and citations are made. Many speech texts suggest the use of notecards to carry out citations. However, with the advent of computers, many speakers, including students, are getting away from storing research material on notecards. The citation and the notes do not change, no matter where you store them.

There are two basic parts to recording your research. First there is the content, that is, the quote, or statistic, or story that you wish to use in the process of building your speech. The other part of researching is getting the citation, which is to say, the location of the material to use in the speech. Do not think of citations as worthless exercises for a grade in speech class. Being able to cite sources gives believability to your speech, helps you to point others to sources, and allows you to go back quickly to sources. The "Bibliography" is the collection of source citations, usually alphabetized according to the source author's last name. Never throw away a good bibliography. That bibliography on "The National Debt" for an informative speech in your freshman or sophomore speech class could be a good starting place for your term paper in your senior economics class.

The rule of thumb for taking notes is to be as complete as possible, while being as concise as possible. Make sure you take down the information you need in order to save time later. If the information includes statistics, make sure you understand and take down the statistical measurements used, the reliability of the statistical tools, and the application of the statistics. A good point to remember is that statistics are only as valuable as their application. If the content you wish to use is a quote of about a sentence or two that is so direct and pointed that you with to use it verbatim, make sure you get every word down correctly. Remember that such direct quotes should be used sparingly and with reference to the author.

The style of citation should be consistent and accurate. Make sure that the page numbers and dates of publication are correct. Here are some examples of citations:

Anderson, Kenneth and Theodore Clevenger. "A Summary of the Experimental Research on Ethos," *Speech Monographs,* 30 (1968), 59–78. (An article in a journal. "30" is the volume number. "59–78" are the page numbers of the article.)

DeVito, Joseph, ed. *Language Concepts and Processes.* Englewood Cliffs, N.J.: Prentice-Hall, 1972. (A book edited by Joseph DeVito, published by Prentice-Hall, a book company.)

Hunt, Gary T. "Listening: Chapter Two." *Public Speaking.* Englewood Cliffs, N.J.: Prentice-Hall, 1981, 11–33. (A chapter in a book, located on pages 11 through 33.)

Organization

Every speech has three basic dimensions of organization: an introduction, a body, and a conclusion. In order to get the three areas well balanced, the speaker organizes the speech by outlining. It is obvious that the introduction gets the speech going, the body gives the bulk of the speech, and the conclusion completes the speech. Although the body of the speech is the longest dimension, the speaker does not want the introduction and conclusion to be so short or long that they are out of balance with the body and with each other.

The basics of outlining are quite simple: *coordination, subordination, and symbol arrangement. Coordination means that two or more points that you wish to place in equal positions in the outline are really equal and parallel.* That is, if they are two equal main points, then they are of equal value in the structure. Suppose you wanted to give a speech on "Types of Suburban Home Structures." You would have several types of homes listed:

A. Colonial
B. Cape Cod
C. Ranch
D. Contemporary

All of these are specific architectural styles. Notice what would happen to the list if you added an element that was not the same:

a. Colonial
b. Cape Cod
c. Ranch
d. Brick

Brick denotes the building material, not the architectural style of the house; therefore, "Brick" is not coordinated with the other subtopics.

Subordination means that each subpoint actually supports the main point. For example, in your effort to explain each type of suburban house type you might include the following:

A. Colonial
   1. Floor plan
   2. Windows
   3. Roofline
B. Cape Cod
   1. Floor plan
   2. Windows
   3. Roofline

Each of the three subpoints, small numbers, under the main points, capital letters, describes or support the main point. Notice how awkward and confusing the following would be:

a. Colonial
   1. Floor plan
   2. Cost
   3. Windows

"Cost" obviously does not support "colonial" if your specific purpose is to inform the audience concerning the types of suburban homes available or currently popular.

The symbol arrangement for outlining helps the speaker in three ways. First, outlining using a formal symbol system gives order or structure to an outline. Second, a formal system assists in keeping the outline in logical sequence. *Last, but not least,* an outlining system is practical, since it is adaptable and applicable to any organizational pattern.

Let's look at a proper outline order:

I.
  A.
     1.
     2.
         a.
         b.

           B.
               1.
               2.
               3.
                   a.
                       1)
                       2)
                           a)
                           b)
                               1]
                               2]
                                   a]
                                   b]
                                       i.
                                       ii.
II. A.
       1.
       2.
           a.
           b.
    B.
       1.
           a.
           b.
       2.
           a.
               1)
               2)
           b.

The system is always in a consistent order.

The logic of outlining is that if there is a Roman numeral "I," then there is a "II." If there is a "A," then there is a "B," and so on. As you may have guessed, the standing rule is that if you have only one subpoint, then you can not have any subpoints. This makes it necessary to decide on the importance of a point which still preparing the speech. This also helps to maintain balance. The introduction of a speech would not have more mainpoints than the body of the speech. The conclusion would also be in balance.

Types of Outline

An outline is really the skeleton or framework of the speech. The speech, as it is presented, is much more than the outlined points. Each speaker, as she gets more experience, will devise a style of outlining. There are three basic types around which you can build a style of outlining: The complete sentence outline, the short phrase outline, and the single word outline.

In the *complete sentence outline,* each point is written out in a complete sentence. Here is a section of a sentence outline on the subject "Why We Should Listen More Effectively":

I. Listening is important in contemporary society.
   A. There are four ways to assess the importance of listening in our lives.
      1. Listening is the first language skill we develop as children.
      2. Listening takes up almost 42 percent of our communication time.
      3. Advanced communication technology has made listening a greater necessity to function in the social, political, and economic life of society.
      4. Listening is the key element in the development of interpersonal relationships.

The *short phrase outline* replaces the full sentence with short phrases of two to several words. The idea is a short hand version of outlining. Here is an example of a short phrase outline, still using our topic on listening:

I. The importance of listening
   A. Four ways to assess importance.
      1. First developed language skill.
      2. Takes 42 percent of communication time.
      3. Technology necessitates listening.
      4. Key element in interpersonal relations.

The *single word outline* is the shortest shorthand of outlining. Each point, main or subpoint, is given only one word. This is the barest skeleton possible, giving meaning only to the speaker who has researched the topic enough to know the subject and the designated subpoints. Let's look at our listening topic as a single word outline.

I. Importance
   A. Assessment
      1. Language
      2. Time
      3. Technology
      4. Relationships

The important factor in outlining is consistency. The style you choose should help you to organize the speech for your presentation. After you choose a type of outline, stick with it consistently while you prepare.

Patterns of Organization

There are five basic patterns of organizing thoughts. Each of these patterns fit into an outline order. The five patterns are topical, chronological, spatial, step, and advantage/disadvantage.

The *topical pattern* is used when the subject divides itself into "topics." Many speeches could be patterned this way. For example, a speech on "Athletics at Our University":

I. Men's athletics
   A. Football
   B. Basketball
   C. Swimming
   D. Baseball
   E. Soccer
II. Women's athletics
   A. Volleyball
   B. Softball
   C. Basketball
   D. Swimming
   E. Gymnastics

The *chronological pattern* arranges the material in time order, that is, what happened first, second, third, and so on. This could be used in any number of speaking topics. For example, a speech on "The History of Sedition Cases in the United States Since 1917" would use the following chronological order:

I. Cases of Sedition in the U.S. from World War I to World War II
   A. Schenck vs. United States, 1919
   B. Abrams vs. United States, 1919
   C. Gitlow vs. New York, 1925
   D. Whitney vs. California, 1927
   E. De Jonge vs. Oregon, 1937
II. Cases of Sedition after the Smith Act of 1940
   A. Dennis vs. United States (1951)
   B. Yates vs. United States (1957)
   C. Brandenburg vs. Ohio (1969)

The *spatial pattern* of organization is effective when the topic has the quality of being separated into physical areas. Spatial, space, arrangement puts information in an order of physical relationship. For example, you could inform the audience of the geographic areas of your state, as this student did, in the topic "South Carolina's Geographic Construct":

I. South Carolina has three main geographic areas that are easily discernable on the map and on the road as you travel through the State.
   A. The coastal region has a distinctive look with wide flat areas with heavy foliage and sandy soil.
   B. The Piedmont, located in the central area of the state, north and west of the coastal area, is marked by rolling hills, less undergrowth, but more deciduous trees.
   C. The Mountain area of the state, located north and west of the Piedmont, is characterized by heavy tree growth and low mountains with wide valleys.

The *step pattern* of organization is based on the idea that some knowledge must be applied in a certain order. When giving instructions the step pattern is very advantageous. Each "step" of the instructions must be performed at a certain time in order for the activity to be successful. Here is an outline instructing students in "How to Drop a Course During Drop-Add":

I. Dropping a course during Drop-Add
   A. Get Drop form from Registrar's office
   B. Fill out form
   C. Get signature of professor of course to be dropped
   D. Get signature of department representative
   E. Take form to Drop-Add division in *Registrar's* office
   F. Keep "Drop Receipt" form mailed to you about one month later.

The *advantage/disadvantage* organizational pattern emphasizes the strong points phase of the general topic over another phase or gives information about a topic or position by a comparison to an alternative. The speaker may not present himself in the role of advocate, because the audience should come away with the feeling of having been given both sides of the question, or issue. The speaker may state the choice he has made, but lets the audience make their own decision. Let's look at an example of the advantage/disadvantage organization in the Speech "Walking is Exercise, Too":

I. Walking is good exercise
   A. Advantages of walking
      1. Inexpensive
      2. Walk anywhere
      3. No special training
      4. Good for cardio-pulmonary system
   B. Disadvantages of walking
      1. Bad weather limits walking
      2. Results take longer
   C. Advantages of walking over running
      1. Fewer foot and leg injuries
      2. Less body stress
      3. No special equipment needed, such as running shoes.

Language and Language Use

Since outlining is just the skeleton of the speech, you are probably now wondering how to put some muscle and skin on those bare bones that make up your outline. You should also wonder how to make the language and organization different to adjust to your audience, or to make your speech more informative or persuasive. First, we should look at some key concepts of presenting oral language to an audience who must hear and listen and not have a chance to get an "instant replay" of the speech.

The language you use for your audience should have some characteristics that make it as easy as possible for the audience to listen and understand. Some good characteristics for language use are

1. clarity
2. conciseness
3. vividness
4. relevance.

Clarity

The language you use should convey, to the best of your ability, what you really mean. One way to insure clarity, or clearness, is to be aware of the many meanings some words have. Avoid using words you know might be misunderstood. Be aware of local usages of words. You might also be aware of the use of words and phrases that might have different meanings to different age groups.

Another way to enhance clarity is to be as concrete as possible. Make a special effort to use realistic examples and illustrations. Especially avoid the abstract because the more abstract you are the less control you have on the visualization process of the audience.

A third way to gain clarity is to avoid jargon, if at all possible. Only use technical terms if there is none to replace them, and then only after you define the term. Jargon, especially abbreviated jargon, is hard to follow. Even if the language sounds impressive, your purpose is not to impress the audience, but to get them to understand.

Conciseness

In your enthusiasm to get a point across, to tell an interesting story, or to explain a difficult concept, you may find yourself deep in a language trap. You will have gone too far, used too many words, even digressed from your original topic. The goal to keep in mind is to be as concise as possible; that is, be economical with language. Too much language will confuse just as much as too little. If you under explain a point, the audience will not understand; if you over explain the audience will stop listening.

Vividness

Language should be clear, concise and interesting. Vividness means that the language will keep the interest of the audience because the words give color and shape to the word pictures you are painting. To do this you should listen to yourself. Do you use the same words over and over? Is your vocabulary limited? Do you use the same phrases over and over? Have you limited yourself by the kinds of phrases and jargon you use? You don't have to learn a number of multi-syllable words to add vividness to your speech. You do have to have variety and a sense of building word pictures.

Relevance

Any language you use should be related to the subject and the audience. The words and language sturctures should indicate an update due the quality and applicability to the audience. If you know you are using a very new term, give a definition so the audience will be knowledgeable. However, make sure that you don't give so many definitions that you appear to be either a "talking" dictionary, which is boring, or condescending to the audience, which is even worse.

Language Use and Speech Purpose

Often a student is overwhelmed at how to "tell" the speech. The beginning speaker sometimes has a problem with how to get the speech started and how to end the speech. We have seen how to do basic organization, so let's look at some crucial problem areas of language and structuring thoughts with language:

1. Beginning the speech
2. Overviews
3. Summaries
4. Ending the speech
5. Special problems with persuasive speeches.

Beginning the Speech

Beginning the speech is hard. However, most student speakers make the mistake of trying to write the beginning of the speech first. A better approach would be to organize and outline the body of the speech and then go back to do the introduction and conclusion. This would mean that you have the pattern already set and know what you are introducing.

How do you actually start a speech? Fortunately, there are a number of ways to start a speech that worked for speakers for years. The introduction of the speech sets the mood or tone for the speech. The introduction should also show the audience that you are a prepared and credible source. In addition to this the introduction should get the audience's attention, because if you don't get their attention in the introduction you may never get it. Here are some ways to start the speech:

1. *Begin with humor.* Good original humor will get a laugh from the audience and set an energetic tone. To get into the speech make sure your humor is humorous before you use it. Jokes that are too old, or that are "inside" jokes, will do more harm than good. Humor that is irrelevant to the subject is only confusing. A true story that is humorous has strong impact with the audience.

2. *Begin with a startling statement.* A statement that is sure to surprise or grab attention is a good way to start a speech, if it is well related to the rest of the speech. The statement should not give away so much of your "punch" that the rest of the speech is boring. Statistics can be used to shake the audience's attention, especially if you feel that the audience has never heard those statistics before.
3. *Begin with an example or story.* A good example of a major point in your speech, or an example that leads to the topic of your speech is a good way to begin. The same is true with a brief story, especially if it is a true story. If the example or the story is hypothetical, let the audience know, after you have given it.
4. *Begin with a quotation.* Quotations can gain attention if they are chosen well and the wording is especially attractive or easy to follow. The quotation does not necessarily have to be from a famous person, but the quote should say something in and of itself. Be sure to give the source of the quotation. Prose, fiction, poetry, drama, and the speeches of others are all good sources for quotations. The writing of historians, philosophers, and newspaper writers can also be valuable. Humorous quotes are also very good. Make sure that the quote in some way can be related to the topic and that the audience will understand.
5. *Begin with a personal reference.* You might have a personal anecdote that would get the audience's attention and draw them into the topic. Another good personal reference would be to give, in a direct but non-broadcasting fashion, any qualifications that make you a good person to approach this topic. If you have personal feelings that justify the necessity of the audience listening to this particular topic, you should make a clear description of your feelings.
6. *Begin with a reference to the audience.* The audience wants to be included; therefore, it would be wise to get their attention by a reference to them. If the topic is of great value to them that would serve as a good starting point. It is always good to make the audience feel important and appreciated.
7. *Begin with a reference to the occasion.* If the audience is gathered for a purpose, it would be good to acknowledge that occasion. For instance, a group gathered together to celebrate a reunion are in a festive mood and would appreciate the reminder. Be sure you understand the nature of the occasion before you tie it in to your speech.
8. *Begin with a reference to the subject.* If your topic is one that is vital, up to date, and in and of itself will get attention, be sure to make mention of it. If you have analyzed your audience well you will know if you have a subject about which the audience has already become enthusiastic.

Notice that I did not mention beginning a speech with a question. A question is a weak way to begin a speech. It assumes a single answer in the audience, or it gets the audience to begin thinking of several answers rather than concentrating on your speech.

Another unfavorable way for starting a speech is to apologize. If you are unprepared the audience will know it, don't forecast their response. If you feel inadequate, you may not really be, so don't put the idea into their minds.

Overview

The introduction of the speech should give a brief overview of the main points of the speech. This comes after you have begun the speech and just before the body of the speech. An overview will get the audience ready to hear the main section of the speech, giving them something to listen for. Do not go into details; that's what the body of the speech is for.

Summaries

After the body of the speech, be sure to restate the main points and summarize just before you end the speech. In this way you will review for the audience so they will better remember your speech. The summary should lead into the ending of the speech: the summary reviews, the ending concludes.

Ending the Speech
1. *End with humor.* Humor is a good beginning and ending. Make sure the humor relates to what has been said and that the audience perceives it as humor.
2. *End with a quotation.* Just as the quotation got the attention of the audience through the quality of language, so does the quote end the speech with a quality of language. If the quote is chosen for its relation to the topic and its wording that brings finality to the speech, it will end the speech well. A quote will not work if it does not relate to the topic or if it leaves the audience hanging.
3. *End with a story.* A good story or short illustration could keep the audience listening and give you a chance to bring the speech to a close. Make sure that the story or illustration is not too long and has a discernable point to it. Don't leave the audience confused or hanging.
4. *End with an appeal.* Ask the audience to action, if that is the outcome of your speech. If you have spent time explaining a problem and its solution to an audience, then ask them to implement that solution. Remind them that if they do take action, they will be able to help solve the problem.
5. *End with a challenge.* Give the audience a challenge, or a goal to meet. This especially works if you have a tried to aspire or motivate during your speech. Tell the audience it is a challenge; then tell them what the challenge is. Make sure the challenge fits the audience; that is, make sure they can do it.

Special Problems with Persuasive Speeches

The persuasive speech has always given the student of public speaking trouble. One obvious way of presenting the speech is an organizational approach that allows for a description of the problem and the presentation of a solution:

A. Problem
   1. Background of problem
   2. Nature of problem
   3. Causes of problem
   4. Effects of problem
B. Solution
   1. Description of solution
   2. How the solution works
   3. Practicality of solution
   4. Advantages of solution

Since this approach might not always work for every persuasive topic, Alan H. Monroe, a professor of speech, developed a step-by-step pattern for persuasive speeches he called the *motivated sequence*. Although Professor Monroe devised this system in the 1930's, students have found that it is especially helpful in beginning and ending the persuasive speech.

The beginning of the motivated sequence is called the *Attention Step*. This means that the speaker uses any of the ways mentioned earlier to get the audience to listen with some interest.

The second step in the sequence is the *need step*, which outlines the problem. This step fully describes the nature and impact of the problem.

The third step, called the *satisfaction step*, is the description of the solution. It is called "satisfaction" because it satisfies the "need," that is, solves the problem.

The fourth step is called the *Visualization step*, which allows the speaker to tell the audience what the situation would be if the solution were to be implemented.

The last step is called the *Action step*. The speaker tells the audience exactly what to do to implement the solution and therefore solve the problem. This is a little different from a challenge. It is a type of appeal, but the speaker is very specific about what she wants the audience to do.

Delivery

You have your speech ready; now you have to prepare to deliver it, that is, to give the speech. There are some basic considerations for presenting the speech.

First, are you going to memorize it, read it, or give it from notes? If you have done preparation you won't be giving it on the spur of the moment, or "off the cuff." This unprepared method is called *impromptu* speaking. When you read a speech, it is called a *manuscript* speech. Persons who are held accountable for every word they say, such as politicians, newscasters, officials of all sorts, read their speech so they won't mis-speak or leave something out. Speeches that are read to an audience lack enthusiasm and spontaneity. The memorized speech begins as a manuscript and is then committed to memory. The *memorized* speech "sounds" memorized, is usually unenthusiastic, and can cause problems if the speaker forgets. The *extemporaneous* speech is the speech that the speaker "knows" rather than has memorized. The speaker usually has some notes, but does not read entirely from them. The extemporaneous speech allows the speaker to get eye contact and show enthusiasm, while maintaining spontaneity.

Building Credibility

Delivery of the speech builds *credibility* for the speaker. The Greeks called credibility *ethos,* meaning the very character of the speaker. We've already looked at some ways to build credibility: know the audience, research the topic, be organized. There are some very specific things you can do to be an effective speaker and build credibility.

1. *Have eye contact with the audience.* Look the audience in the eyes. Never look over their heads, and never, never out the window. Try not to be tied to your notes; this makes it seem that you don't "know" what you are talking about. Try to get eye contact with all the audience.
2. *Speak loudly enough to be heard.* A too soft voice seems unsure. If the audience is straining, they aren't focusing on what you are saying.
3. *Articulate your words, using good pronunciation.* Articulation refers to your ability to clearly make the sounds of the language. Pronunciation means that you are able to use accepted accents and stresses within words. If you are unsure of the pronunciation of a word, look it up in a dictionary. Listen to yourself on a tape recorder to hear any patterns of articulation or pronunciation problems that you can change.
4. *Work for good voice quality.* Although you were given only one voice box, you can try to improve. Do you speak too low in pitch to be understood? Is your voice so high and thin others think of you as an "air head?" Work on a pleasing sound for your voice.
5. *Use gestures when you speak.* Too many movements are distracting, but no movements are boring. Do not pace when you speak, but don't be afraid to move, if you are comfortable doing it and it helps relate to the audience without distracting. If you are stuck at a microphone, remember that your face, upper body, arms and hands speak with you. Notice yourself in a mirror. Try to get feedback from others.

6. *Be confident of yourself.* You are the only one of you there is, so use your uniqueness to help your delivery. Never apologize for who you are or how you look. Think of yourself as a public speaker and soon you will be one.
7. *Get experience speaking.* Never turn down an offer to speak! Think of it as an opportunity rather than a burden. The more experience you have the easier it will be to speak. You will never be completely free of anxiety or "nerves," but you will look forward to the public speaking situation without dread. Remember, you are not just speaking; you are communicating.

Instructional Exercises

1. Write down everything you already know about your communication class. Organize the information as an audience analysis.
2. Think of three topics that you know you can speak for one minute on without research. Choose one of those topics and prepare three minutes of information.
3. Tape record yourself reading the newspaper for five minutes. Make a list of what you would change about your voice. Give the list to your instructor.
4. Read the newspaper. Find a story of interest to you. Prepare a five minute speech with an Introduction, Body, and Conclusion. Present it as an extemporaneous speech to your class.
5. Find a problem on campus or in your town that has a solution that you think will work. Using Monroe's motivated sequence, prepare an 8–minute persuasive speech. Give it to the class.

Additional Readings

Bradley, Bert E. *Fundamentals of Speech Communication: The Credibility of Ideas,* 4th edition. Dubuque, Iowa: Wm. C. Brown Company Publishers, 1984.

Kulgren, J. A. "The Effects of Organization upon the Comprehension of a Persuasive-Type Speech," M.A. thesis, Fresno State College, Calif., 1960.

Spicer, C. and Bassett, R. E. "The Effect of Organization on Learning from an Informative Message." *Southern Speech Communication Journal* 41 (1976).

Miller, E. "Speech Introduction and Conclusions." *Quarterly Journal of Speech* 32 (1946):181–83.

Index

Adaptors, 17
Advantages, 55
Advantages/disadvantages outline, 94
Affect Displays, 17, 18
Affection, 28
Appreciative listening, 11
Arbitrariness, 8
Argot, 9
Articulation, 21
Assertiveness, 31, 32, 33
Attitudes, 60
Audience Analysis, 84

Barnard, Chester I., 71
Beginning the speech, 96
Birdwhistell, Ray, 16
Brainstorming, 60

Cant, 9
Chronological pattern outline, 93
Citations, 89
Clarity, 95
Cliche communication, 35, 36
Climate, 33
Common ground, 85
Comparison levels, 26
Complementary relationship, 28
Complete Sentence outline, 92
Compromise, 25
Conciseness, 95
Connotative meanings, 10
Control, 28
Credibility, 100

Data, 88
Decision-making, 56
    intuition, 56
    outcomes, 57
    risk-taking, 56, 57
    values, 58
Defensiveness, 34
Delivery, 99
Denotative meanings, 10
Dewey, John, 58
Discriminative listening, 11
Displacement, 8

Economic View of relationship, 25, 26
Ego involvement, 61
Emblems, 17
Emotional communication, 35
Empathic listening, 11
Endicott, Frank, 46
Ending the speech, 98

Ethos, 100
Evaluative listening, 11

Factual communication, 35
Functions of small group, 54
    group definition, 53

Hall, E. T., 18
Hearing, 10
Homans, G. C., 26

Illustrators, 18
Inclusion, 27, 28
Information sharing, 54
Informative versus persuasive speaking, 87
Initiation, 53
Interview, 41–49
    approaches to, 42
        duological, 42
        polylogical, 42
    definition of, 42
    legal restrictions in, 47, 48
    roles in, 45
        interviewee, 42
        interviewer, 42
        questions, 45
    sequences, 45
        funnel, 45
        inverted funnel, 45
    types of, 43
        employment, 45, 46, 47
        information gathering, 43, 44
Intimate space, 20

Jargon, 8
Judgmental communication, 35

Kahn, Robert L., 71
Katz, Daniel, 71
Kinesthetic factors, 18

Language in public speaking, 94, 95, 96
Latitude of acceptance, 61
Leadership, 61
Listening, 10–12
Loudness, 21

March, James G., 71
Maturation, 53
Mayo, Elton, 71
Miller, James G., 71
Monroe, Alan H., 99
Motivated sequence, 99

Object adaptors, 17
Ogden, C. K. and Richards, I. A., 9
Olson, Johan P., 71
Organizational behavior, 71, 72
    approaches to, 71
        human relations, 71
        scientific management, 71
        symbolic, 71
        systems, 71
Organizational communication, 73
    barriers to, 77
        physical, 77
        physiological, 77
        psychological, 77
        semantic, 77
    definition of, 73
    formal, 75
        downward, 75
        lateral, 75
        upward, 75
    informal, 75
        grapevine, 75
        serial transmission, 75
    symbolic, 76
        action, 76
        material, 76
        verbal, 76
    techniques for improving, 78
Organizational socialization, 71, 72
    definition of, 72
    stages of, 72
        arrival, 72
        post-arrival, 72
        pre-arrival, 72
Organizations, 69, 70
    definition of, 69
    perspectives of, 70
        counterrational, 70
        rational, 70
Outlining, 89
    coordination, 89
    logic, 91
    subordination, 90
    symbol arrangement, 90
Overviews, 98

Paralinguistics, 20
Parallel relationship, 29, 30
Patterns of organization, 92, 94
Peak communication, 35
Personal distance, 20

Phonation, 21
Pitch, 21
Postural-sex identifiers, 18
Powell, T., 35
Problem-solving, 54, 58
Public distance, 20

Rate, 21
Reference, 9
Referent, 9
Reflective thinking, 59
Relevance of language, 96
Resonance, 21
Role conflict, 63, 64
Roles, 62
Role set, 62, 63

Schutz, W., 27
Secrets, 37
Self-disclosure, 34, 35, 36, 37
Short Phrase outline, 92
Simon, Herbert A., 71
Single word outline, 92
Slang, 9
Smell, 19
Social distance, 20
Social exchange, 26
Socioemotional functions, 61
Sociofugal-sociopetal orientation, 18
Spatial pattern, 93
Springbett, B. M., 46
Step pattern, 94
Summaries, 98
Supportiveness, 14
Symbol, 9
Symmetrical relationship, 29, 30

Task functions, 61
Taylor, Frederick W., 71
Team building, 55
Tempo, 21
Thermal Factors, 19
Topical pattern outline, 93
Touch, 19

Vision, 19
Vividness of language, 95
Vocal segregates, 21
Volume, 21

Wanous, J. P., 46
Weick, Karl E., 71

Listening is not a passive position but a **powerful** one

Perception — people focus on info that is reinforcing of their frame of reference (filters) or rewarding.

We tend to see things the way we are used to seeing them & accustomed to expecting things to be

Maturity is doing whatever is possible to help persons maintain healthy self-concepts

Self-talk is healthy — intrapersonal

Real Self vs Ideal Self

Listening or Receiving
requires the ability to be impacted by others. You have to loosen the reigns of control & let yourself change.

It is a physic or psycho/physical phenomenna

Hearing is physiological
Listening is under<u>standing</u> —
Does this mean you have to take the em. energy in & ground it thru your body?

Empathic Listening — Key is to give time with an open mind.
<s>For me</s> it requires a <u>neutral position rather than defensive stance</u>.

If you want me to receive don't blame me.

Train – Verbal & Non Verbal Comm.

Listening

How to Be Still

Vocal Qualities that aid meaning & receptivity
R B Y   to change intended meaning
the characteristics of the voice used also give meaning

Team Spirit – Making each person feel respected & valued

Create a Climate or Atmosphere for good communication

~~Group leadership~~
let the best qualified
be the leader at a given time
TASK LEADER

Let people know you care
about them as well as
their performance

Levels of Comm. Peak
(of self-disclosure) Emotional
Judgmental
Factual
Cliché